PENGUIN BUSINESS
MASTERING DISRUPTION

K. Ganesh is a seasoned serial entrepreneur and the founder of GrowthStory.in, a leading venture builder platform that has incubated and scaled multiple successful start-ups across diverse sectors, including BigBasket, Portea Medical, Bluestone and HomeLane, which have redefined industries by leveraging innovative business models and cutting-edge technologies.

Ganesh's entrepreneurial journey also includes founding and scaling ventures like IT&T (acquired by iGate), CustomerAsset (acquired by ICICI, now known as FirstSource), Marketics (acquired by NASDAQ-listed WNS) and TutorVista (acquired by Pearson).

An adjunct professor at Indian Institute of Management (IIM) Bangalore, Ganesh teaches courses on new-age Business Models, bringing his extensive experience in disruptive technologies and management to the classroom. A mentor to start-ups and an active angel investor, Ganesh has been instrumental in shaping India's start-up ecosystem.

He is a distinguished alumnus of Indian Institute of Management (IIM) Calcutta and Delhi University, a frequent speaker at global forums and a champion of social initiatives in healthcare and skill development through his non-profit, Bahaar Foundation.

This book reflects his deep understanding of the transformative business models shaping the future of industries worldwide.

ADVANCE PRAISE FOR THE BOOK

'India is amid an entrepreneurial renaissance, driven by digital public infrastructure, innovation and an increasingly connected global economy. *Mastering Disruption* offers a comprehensive lens on how new-age business models can harness these opportunities to build scalable and inclusive enterprises. This book is an essential read for entrepreneurs, policymakers and business leaders aiming to thrive in a rapidly evolving economic landscape. Drawing from K. Ganesh's remarkable track record of building successful ventures, the book provides both strategic insights and practical guidance'— **Nandan Nilekani, co-founder and chairman, Infosys and founding chairman, UIDAI**

'In *Mastering Disruption*, K. Ganesh decodes the future of finance, making this book indispensable for anyone delivering innovation at scale and leveraging technology for growth. It is an essential read for anyone interested in the topic'—**Vijay Shekhar Sharma, founder and CEO, Paytm**

'Serial entrepreneur and successful investor K. Ganesh's new-age business models is one of the highly acclaimed courses in the IIM Bangalore MBA curriculum. I am delighted to see that his cutting-edge insights will now be available to a wider audience through *Mastering Disruption*'—**Rishikesha T. Krishnan, director, IIM Bangalore**

'K. Ganesh has brilliantly captured the essence of on-demand innovation in *Mastering Disruption*. A must-read for anyone shaping the future of commerce and service delivery'—**Sriharsha Majety, CEO and co-founder, Swiggy**

MASTERING DISRUPTION

A PRACTICAL GUIDE TO UNDERSTANDING

NEW—AGE BUSINESS MODELS

K. GANESH

PENGUIN
BUSINESS

An imprint of Penguin Random House

PENGUIN BUSINESS

Penguin Business is an imprint of the Penguin Random House group of companies whose addresses can be found at global.penguinrandomhouse.com

Published by Penguin Random House India Pvt. Ltd
4th Floor, Capital Tower 1, MG Road,
Gurugram 122 002, Haryana, India

Penguin
Random House
India

First published in Penguin Business by Penguin Random House India 2025

Copyright © K. Ganesh 2025

All rights reserved

10 9 8 7 6 5 4

The views and opinions expressed in this book are the author's own and the facts are as reported by him which have been verified to the extent possible, and the publishers are not in any way liable for the same.

Please note that no part of this book may be used or reproduced in any manner for the purpose of training artificial intelligence technologies or systems.

ISBN 9780143474500

Typeset in Bembo Std by MAP Systems, Bengaluru, India
Printed at Replika Press Pvt. Ltd, India

www.penguin.co.in

MIX
Paper | Supporting
responsible forestry
FSC™ C016779

To my mother, my unwavering role model and inspiration.

Widowed at the age of thirty-five, you raised three young children with immense strength, grace and resilience. You ensured that we never felt a sense of lack, all the while instilling in us the enduring values of hard work, positivity and gratitude.

This book is a tribute to your remarkable spirit and unconditional love.

Contents

Preface

The world of business is undergoing a seismic shift. What worked yesterday may not work today, and what works today may be obsolete tomorrow. We are witnessing the rapid emergence of business models that are redefining industries, challenging norms and creating unprecedented opportunities for value creation. From the subscription revolution to platform economies, direct-to-consumer models and the creator economy, this era is rich with innovation—and complexity.

As an entrepreneur and investor who has had the privilege of building and scaling disruptive ventures across sectors, I have been both a participant and a keen observer of this transformation. My journey—from founding and running ventures such as IT&T, FirstSource, Marketics and TutorVista to promoting companies such as BigBasket, BlueStone, Portea Medical and HomeLane—has offered me a front-row seat to the ever-evolving dynamics of business and technology. This experience, coupled with my roles as a mentor, angel investor and educator at IIM Bangalore and the Indian School of Business, has helped me distil key lessons that I believe are invaluable for navigating today's business landscape.

This book was born out of a simple yet profound need: to make sense of this change. It aims to serve as a compass for entrepreneurs, managers, students, investors and curious readers alike. Whether you are a seasoned professional adapting to digital transformation, a budding entrepreneur shaping your own path or a student eager to grasp the future of commerce, this book is designed to equip you with insights, strategies and tools for success.

Through its chapters, it explores the fundamental shifts that have redefined business models. It examines the difference between traditional pipeline models and new-age platform ecosystems, unpacks key metrics that define modern businesses and dives deep into sectors experiencing tectonic shifts, such as SaaS, fintech and direct-to-consumer brands. Real-world examples, coupled with actionable frameworks, provide a clear understanding of how to innovate, adapt and thrive.

At its core, *Mastering Disruption* is more than a guide to new-age business models—it is a call to embrace change. The velocity of disruption can feel daunting but within it lies boundless potential. Companies that understand and harness the dynamics of this new world will not only survive but flourish. Similarly, individuals who develop a keen grasp of these concepts will find themselves ahead of the curve, equipped to lead, innovate and succeed.

As you embark on this journey through the pages of this book, my hope is that you will find not only knowledge but inspiration. The future is being written today, and every business, every professional, has the opportunity to be a part of that story. Let's embrace the disruption, understand it and master it.

Foreword

Disruption is something that forces a change in your daily routine. This is true for an individual, a team, a company and an industry. The automobile disrupted the horse carriage, the train disrupted the stagecoach. Examples are plentiful, and today, the pace of disruption is faster than ever.

The average lifespan of a company was ninety years in 1930 and sixty years in 1960. Today, it ranges between twelve and eighteen years, depending on the database you consult. Thirty-three per cent of Fortune 500 companies disappear from the list every decade, which means seventeen companies are lost each year, or about 1.5 companies vanish every month. That's staggering!

The reason—disruption and a failure to recognize, along with the inability to stay ahead by fine-tuning the business model. The speed of disruption is baffling, and technology turns every firm ground of the past into a quicksand pit. Technology also forces every company to think of the ecosystem they belong to. In the mobile phone business, there are two ecosystems today—iOS and Android. Nokia went from being a global leader in 2010 to an also-ran by 2014 because the app ecosystem took off, and Nokia failed to bet on the right operating system. Worse, they chose the worst one—Windows—leaving them with little chance of success.

Everyone thinks they know what's happening in their industry, but their perspective is often shaped by current industry players and practices. A digital experience allows consumers to engage with products and services in a completely different way. In India, consumers shop digitally, watch entertainment digitally, book tickets digitally, and have their income tax returns approved and refunded within days. That's the experience the consumer expects when he deals with every category and company. Sadly, many companies are stuck in past physical model thinking and are therefore losing. The FMCG sector is a prime example of this ostrich mentality.

History tells us that disruption comes mostly from outside the current industry ecosystem and players. Tesla, with its EVs challenging ICE cars, and BYD, transitioning from cell phone batteries to EV cars, are prime examples. No auto manager in the USA, Europe or China saw that coming.

When confronted with disruption, the only choice before a business is 'embracing change or protecting legacy'. With disruption comes a business model change, every business model changes the price value equation in the industry first and then the profit pool shifts. Many legacy-protecting companies start by cutting prices, and before long, their balance sheets are in the red.

The term 'business model' has existed since 1832, and every few decades, we have new business models cropping up. A business model is simply the way a company creates and captures value. In a sense, it's an end-to-end game. There are value-creation opportunities in sourcing, making, moving and selling a product or service. In the past, business models were defined by 'physicality'; in the digital world, they are defined by the digital experience. Over time, the sources of creation and the places of consumption have increasingly moved apart.

Technology and smartphones have given rise to platform models across every industry. These models rely on advertising, monetizing information, upselling and creating seamless experiences.

India is a data-rich and digital stack-rich country. Innovation and experimentation in digital business models are exponential here and will continue to grow. The simple Aadhaar card finds its way into nearly every model. Matrimonial sites, for instance, now offer 'Aadhaar-verified' candidates for brides and grooms.

Ganesh has been a friend since college. We've kept in touch over the years, and he taught the new-age business models course at IIM Bangalore. He invited me to take a few sessions in his course, and we also recorded three hours of content in the IIM Bangalore studio on disruption and business models. Ganesh is a serial entrepreneur who has witnessed first-hand the development of business models and platform business models in India. There is no one better suited to write this book on new-age business models. I consider it a privilege to write the foreword for this book.

Before I sign off, I want to share the story of Dick Fosbury and would request you to look for the Dick Fosburys in your company. Dick Fosbury was an American high jumper. He went to his coach in the 1960s and said that he would like to do the high jump with his back clearing the high jump bar. The coach did not stop him, and Dick Fosbury went on to win the Olympic gold in 1968. To this day, everyone uses the Fosbury Flop. Encourage your people to think differently, and you will master disruption and develop unique business models.

Shiv Shivakumar
business leader, author and ex-chairman,
PepsiCo India and ex-CEO,
Emerging Markets
January 2025
Gurgaon

1

An Overview of Various Business Models

As per popular legend, in 1997, Reed Hastings, a software entrepreneur, was fined $40 at his local video store for returning the DVD of the movie *Apollo 13* late. This unpleasant experience got him thinking: there has to be a better business model for video rentals. He started Netflix, a DVD-by-mail service with no late fees, which was later transformed into a subscription-based online streaming service. Today, Netflix is a global behemoth in the entertainment industry, all thanks to a business model that was born out of a sense of personal frustration.

In India, a man named Arunachalam Muruganantham embarked on a mission to produce affordable sanitary pads for the women in his village. His business model was built around empowering rural women, not just by providing access to affordable sanitary products but also by offering them an opportunity to earn a living. His company, Jayaashree Industries, supplied semi-automatic machines to women-led self-help groups who produced and sold the pads, turning a societal challenge into an entrepreneurial opportunity. This model has been hailed as a breakthrough in socially conscious business innovation.

At the dawn of the twentieth century, the Ford Motor Company revolutionized the automobile industry not just through the invention of the assembly line but also through an innovative business model. Henry Ford's vision of making a car for the great multitude required a drastic reduction in prices, which led to the development of a business model based on cost efficiencies and economies of scale. This story serves as a classic example of how business model innovation can drive growth and disrupt industries.

All these examples show that business models are not static; they are dynamic and change with time. They are not set in stone; they need to evolve with changing market conditions and customer needs.

Did you know that each year, more than half of the Fortune 500 companies have to innovate their business models to stay on the list? A business model that worked in the past might not be successful in the future, and companies that fail to innovate their business models risk being left behind.

Business Model

So, what is a business model? In simple terms, it is a conceptual structure that supports the viability of a business and explains how it operates and makes money, and how it intends to achieve its goals. More importantly, a business model encapsulates the value proposition for customers—that unique cocktail of products, services and experiences that make a business stand out from the crowd.

Imagine walking into a bustling marketplace filled with vendors, each trying to outshine the others, vying for your attention and your hard-earned money. Their strategies for enticing you differ significantly—one offers a subscription for a basket of fresh produce every week, another entices you with a bundle of complementary products at a discounted rate, a third proposes a franchise model to help you set up your own thriving business, and yet another offers the convenience of on-demand service, where you get what you want, when you want it. All of these are business models in action, strategically designed to create, deliver and capture value.

An Examination of Traditional Business Models

We begin our exploration of business models by examining the conventional, time-honoured structures that have enabled businesses to create and capture value throughout history. Each model has its own distinctive strengths, weaknesses and unique elements, which need to be grasped for achieving business success. It's worth noting that these models are not mutually exclusive and can often be interwoven and amalgamated.

Manufacturer Business Model:

This model involves the creation of products from raw materials or component parts by a company. The products can be sold directly to consumers, or through an intermediary.

Example: Tata Motors exemplifies this model, designing and manufacturing an array of vehicles sold via their dealer network.

Ford Motor Company represents this model on a global scale, selling its extensive range of vehicles through worldwide distribution channels.

Strengths and weaknesses: The manufacturing model offers control over production, quality and pricing. Higher volumes can lead to economies of scale, reducing costs and increasing profitability. However, high initial costs, continuous maintenance expenses and potential supply chain complexities can be challenges. The ability to change the established infrastructure to match evolving market dynamics and consumer preferences can also be a hurdle.

Distributor Business Model:

Here, an intermediary (the distributor) acquires products from manufacturers and sells them to retailers or consumers.

Example: Redington India exemplifies this model as a leading distributor of Information Technology and mobility products, sourcing them from top manufacturers and selling them to a broad network of retailers and consumers. Ingram Micro is a global technology distributor and solutions provider that operates in over 100 countries.

Strengths and weaknesses: Distributors can negotiate pricing with both manufacturers and retailers, potentially enhancing profits. However, they may face vulnerability to supply–demand fluctuations and the challenge of maintaining efficient logistics and warehousing. They also risk being superseded by new distributors or circumvented by manufacturers selling directly to consumers or through e-commerce platforms.

Retailer Business Model:

Retailers purchase products from manufacturers or distributors and sell them to end consumers via bricks-and-mortar stores or e-commerce platforms.

Example: Reliance Retail, which operates convenience stores, supermarkets and speciality stores under various brands such as JioMart, Reliance Jewels, Fresh Signature, Reliance Trends, etc. exemplifies this model.

Walmart, the world's largest retailer, sells a diverse range of products sourced from various manufacturers and distributors through thousands of its stores.

Strengths and weaknesses: Retailers can gain insights from direct consumer contact, negotiate enticing deals with brands and leverage hyperlocal access to promote preferred brands and products. However, challenges can include inventory management, fluctuating consumer demand, competition and the costs of maintaining retail infrastructure. They also operate on low gross margins.

Franchise Business Model:

In this model, an individual or company (the franchisee) purchases the rights to use a company's (the franchisor's) brand name, operating methods and product knowledge to sell to consumers.

Example: BlueStone and ChaiPoint are Indian companies using this model, operating through a network of franchisee-owned stores. McDonald's is a renowned franchise business, with the majority of its outlets globally owned and operated by franchisees.

Strengths and weaknesses: Franchising enables rapid expansion with less capital required to be invested by the franchisor, who can focus on brand-building, product development and system standardization, while franchisees manage capital investment and daily operations. However, maintaining brand standards across all franchises can be challenging.

Contract Manufacturing Business Model:

This involves outsourcing certain parts of the production process of a business to a third-party company.

Contract manufacturing can be a valuable option for businesses of all sizes that are looking to outsource the production of their products.

Examples: Foxconn, Flextronics and Yue Yuen are some large contract manufacturing companies that work with top brands like Apple, Samsung and Nike.

Strengths and weaknesses: This model allows for concentration on core competencies such as product development, marketing and sales, while the contract manufacturer takes care of the manufacturing process. It reduces investment in production facilities and can lower production costs. However, it may lead to less control over production quality, potential intellectual property issues and geopolitical risks.

Licensing Business Model:

Licensing involves granting a company or individual the right to use a business's product, brand, patent, technology or other assets for a fee or royalty.

Examples: Disney licenses its characters and brands to a wide range of products and services, including toys, clothing, food and video games. Marvel is a comic book publisher that has licensed its characters and brands to a wide range of products, including movies, television shows and video games. Star Wars is a science fiction franchise that has been licensed to a wide range of products, including movies, television shows and video games.

Strengths and weaknesses: Licensing enables companies to monetize their assets with minimal investment, mitigate risks and access new markets. However, it can involve a loss of control over the asset, risk of inferior reproductions and potential damage to the brand reputation.

Razor-Blade Business Model:

Under this model, companies sell a one-time product at a low price, but the product requires frequent purchases of related products.

Examples: Gillette, Hewlett–Packard (printers and ink).

Strengths and weaknesses: This model generates recurring revenue and promotes customer loyalty. However, it requires consistent purchase of consumables to be profitable, and the initial product may be sold at a loss or very low margins.

Leasing Business Model:

In this model, a company retains ownership of an asset and rents it to customers for a periodic fee.

Example: Cat Financials, the financial services arm of Caterpillar Inc., the world's largest manufacturer of construction and mining equipment, provides an operating lease of its equipment to customers instead of selling them outright. Similarly, several automotive manufacturers lease the vehicles to customers and car rental agencies.

Strengths and weaknesses: This model provides customers access to high-cost assets and a steady revenue to companies. However, maintenance and replacement costs are to be borne by the company, and revenue depends on high utilization rates.

Bundling Business Model:

Companies sell multiple products or services together as a package, often at a lower price than if they had been sold separately. This is often done to increase the order value or to push slow-moving products.

Example: Airtel broadband and digital TV combo, Zomato Pro Plus (deliveries + dining), Office Suite, McDonald's meal deals (Combo Meal + Fries + Beverage).

Strengths and weaknesses: This model can increase the sales volume, move unsold inventory and deliver greater value to customers. It uses the strength of one product to push a weaker or newer product and to induce trial. There is a risk that the perceived value of individual products may be lowered, and customers may feel forced to buy items they do not want.

An Exploration of New-age Business Models

As the business environment continues to evolve, we see a shift in how companies structure their operations to create and capture value. Let us explore new-age business models, highlighting their unique characteristics and the opportunities they present to contemporary enterprises.

Platform Business Model:

This model revolves around a digital platform that serves as a conduit for transactions between independent parties—usually consumers and producers. Generally, platform operators own neither the production or the consumption assets, but they profit from coordinating interactions or transactions.

Example: Airbnb stands as an archetype, providing a platform where property owners (hosts) and travellers (guests) connect and conduct business.

Strengths and weaknesses: The platform model gains from network effects—the platform's value escalates as more people use it. However, this model requires significant initial investment and effort to attract users, and it can be susceptible to regulatory challenges. Platforms need to ensure that all participants derive value and continue using the platform, making the monetization of interactions a challenging task.

Aggregator Business Model:

The aggregator model consolidates specific services or products and offers them under a single brand. The aggregator itself doesn't provide the service or product but connects service providers with consumers.

Example: Urban Company operates as an aggregator that links skilled professionals with users requiring home-based services, ranging from beauty treatments to appliance repair. Ola Cabs, connecting independent drivers with ride-seekers, also employs this model.

Strengths and weaknesses: The aggregator model allows quick scaling without owning assets but needs a substantial user base to succeed; the challenge is that attracting both sides can be difficult. Ensuring continued use of the platform to avoid disintermediation is vital.

On-demand Business Model:

In this model, businesses leverage technology to meet customer needs immediately or at short notice.

Example: Swiggy, an online food delivery platform, epitomizes the on-demand model, delivering food from restaurants to customers swiftly upon order.

Strengths and weaknesses: On-demand businesses can deliver high levels of customer satisfaction due to their convenience. However, they may face logistical challenges and fluctuating demand. To fulfil orders, the company must ensure sufficient capacity at all times, leading to possible underutilization and consequent losses.

Subscription-based Business Model:

While subscriptions aren't a new concept, modern businesses have adapted this model for digital services and products.

Example: Hotstar, a digital and mobile entertainment platform, offers a diverse range of TV shows, movies and live sports under a subscription model.

Strengths and weaknesses: This model ensures predictable recurring revenue but may struggle with customer acquisition and retention, as low upfront commitments can lead to high customer turnover.

Direct-to-Consumer (D2C) Business Model:

In the D2C model, companies sell their products directly to consumers, eliminating intermediaries like retailers, wholesalers or distributors.

Example: Lenskart, an eyewear brand, uses a D2C model, selling eyewear directly to consumers via its website and app.

Strengths and weaknesses: D2C allows higher profit margins and access to better customer data but necessitates investments in brand-building and logistics management.

Creator Economy Business Model:

The Creator Economy represents a new economic paradigm where anyone can create, share content online and monetize it, thanks to social media platforms. Creators can make money in many different ways, selling physical goods, digital goods, affiliate marketing, brand sponsorships or even subscriptions from followers.

Example: YouTube is a video-sharing platform that allows users to watch, upload and share videos. Twitch is a live streaming platform that allows users to watch and interact with live video broadcasts. Instagram is a photo- and video-sharing platform that allows users to share their photos and videos with their followers. Moj is a short-form video app that allows users to create and share videos.

Strengths and weaknesses: This model democratizes value creation and enables individual entrepreneurship. However, competition can be fierce.

Consumer-to-Consumer (C2C) Business Model:

The C2C model enables commerce between private individuals, usually facilitated by a third-party platform.

Example: eBay provides a platform for individuals to buy and sell goods.

Strengths and weaknesses: This model eliminates the need for a physical storefront, reducing costs and expanding market reach. However, it can face issues with trust, security and product or service quality control.

Freemium Business Model:

In the freemium model, basic services are provided free of charge, while more advanced features or services require payment.

Example: LinkedIn offers basic professional networking services for free, but charges for advanced features. Zoom provides free basic video conferencing facilities for a limited time but charges a fee for greater usage.

Strengths and weaknesses: This model can attract a large user base and converting some of them into paying customers is easy, but converting the free users into paying customers can be challenging.

Crowdsourcing Business Model:

Here, companies solicit ideas, services or content from a large group of people, usually an online community.

Example: Kickstarter operates on the basis of this model, allowing people to fund projects or ideas.

Strengths and weaknesses: The model allows access to a wide range of talents and ideas, often at a lower cost. However, quality can vary, and managing a diverse crowd can be challenging.

SuperApp Model:

A SuperApp is a mobile application that provides multiple functions and services within a single app.

Example: WeChat serves as a prime global example, offering various services from messaging and social media to online shopping and payments. Tata Neu App is another example in which users can buy anything from grocery, medicines and electronics to hotel reservations seamlessly, while earning loyalty points that can be used across verticals.

Strengths and weaknesses: SuperApps are convenient for users and can leverage data across services for better personalization. However, their development and maintenance can be complex, and quality issues due to the broad range of services can impact user perception.

Hybrid Business Models

Hybrid business models intertwine elements of traditional and modern models to create unique value propositions tailored to a company's specific needs and the market dynamics. The effectiveness of these hybrid models often lies in their adaptability and resilience, allowing businesses to pivot, based on shifting customer demands and market trends.

Direct-to-Consumer with Physical Retail:

In this hybrid model, businesses primarily operate on a direct-to-consumer model, selling products online directly to consumers, but they also operate physical retail stores.

Lenskart, an eyewear brand, initially started as a D2C online platform. Over time, it has integrated a physical retail component by opening bricks-and-mortar stores, providing customers with the flexibility of online shopping and the personal touch of in-store experiences.

Warby Parker, a US-based eyewear brand, started as a purely online D2C business but has since then expanded into physical retail with a network of stores across the country. Customers can browse frames online and try them at home or visit a physical store for a more personalized experience.

Strengths and weaknesses: This hybrid model benefits from the broad reach and efficiency of online D2C selling and the tangible, personal experience provided by physical retail. However, it also inherits the challenges of both models, including managing logistics and inventory for online sales and the high operational costs associated with physical stores.

Marketplace + Private Label:

In this model, companies operate as an online marketplace, facilitating transactions between independent sellers and customers, while also selling their own private label products.

Flipkart, India's leading e-commerce platform, operates on this hybrid model. On the one hand, it acts as a marketplace where numerous independent sellers can list and sell their products. On the other, it sells its own private label products, such as 'MarQ' for electronics and appliances, SmartBuy for accessories and Cara Mia, a fashion brand that offers a range of women's clothing, including dresses, skirts and tops. Amazon, a global e-commerce behemoth, operates as a marketplace hosting millions of independent sellers while selling its own private label products across a range of categories, from electronics to apparel.

Strengths and weaknesses: This model benefits from the broad reach and variety of a marketplace, coupled with the higher profit margins that come from selling private label products. However, it also inherits the challenges of managing a vast seller network, maintaining product quality and dealing with potential conflicts between the marketplace and private label operations.

D2C + Retailer Model:

In this hybrid model, companies sell their own products directly to consumers and sell other popular brands, acting as retailers.

Nykaa, an Indian beauty and fashion retailer, exemplifies this model. It sells its own beauty products directly to consumers under the Nykaa brand, and also operates as a retailer, selling a range of international and Indian beauty brands on its platform as well as its retail stores on the high street.

Strengths and weaknesses: This model leverages the higher profit margins and brand-building benefits of D2C, while also offering the variety and customer reach of a retail operation. The challenges include managing logistics for both models, building and maintaining a brand and managing potential competition between their own products and those of other brands on their platform. The potential cannibalization of their customer base and confused customer perception are other challenges.

Content Producer + Streaming Platform:

This model combines the roles of content production and distribution. Companies produce their own content and also distribute content from other producers.

Netflix is a quintessential example of this model. It produces a slew of original content under the Netflix Originals banner while also hosting and streaming content from other production companies.

Strengths and weaknesses: This model provides control over some of the content, allowing for unique offerings and differentiation, while also benefiting from the variety of hosting external content. However, it requires significant investment in content production and faces the challenges of managing content rights and handling competition from other streaming platforms.

In summary, these hybrid models illustrate that by integrating various business models, companies can reap the benefits of each model while mitigating their individual weaknesses. Nonetheless, it is vital to remember that a hybrid model's effectiveness depends heavily on specific factors such as customer behaviour, competitive landscape, regulatory environment and the company's core competencies.

Business Model Innovation

In an era of rapid technological progress and shifting market dynamics, business model innovation has become a critical strategic lever for companies to stay competitive. Business model innovation refers to the process of fundamentally rethinking your business around a clear—often disruptive—customer offering and a robust operating model that can support that customer promise.

This is different from product innovation or process innovation, which focuses on creating new products or improving existing processes, respectively. Business model innovation, on the other hand, involves redefining the way a company creates, delivers and captures value.

Successful Business Model Innovation Examples

Reliance Jio: Reliance Jio disrupted the Indian telecommunications industry with its business model innovation. Instead of simply competing on price or quality, Jio was launched with a radical offering: free voice calls and ultra-cheap data services. This brought millions of users onto their platform, leading to rapid scale and enabling Jio to monetize other aspects such as content services, creating a new business model in the Indian telecom industry.

Zerodha: Zerodha, an Indian financial services company, innovated the brokerage model in India by introducing a flat fee 'discount' model, vastly undercutting traditional brokers who charged a percentage of the trade value. This made trading accessible to a broader segment of the population and allowed Zerodha to rapidly gain market share.

Netflix: Netflix started as a DVD rental service, which was a successful business model at the time. However, foreseeing the rise of the Internet and changing consumer habits, Netflix pivoted to a subscription-based online streaming model. It later added a new layer of innovation by investing in original content, further distinguishing itself from other streaming platforms.

Apple: Apple transformed the music industry with the introduction of iTunes and the iPod. Instead of selling CDs, Apple sold individual songs digitally, meeting the changing needs of consumers and disrupting the existing business model in the music industry. Later, Apple innovated again by shifting from a transactional model (buying each song) to a subscription model with Apple Music.

Failed Business Model Innovation Examples

Kodak: Despite being a pioneer in digital photography, Kodak failed to adapt its business model to the digital revolution. It stuck to its film-based business model for too long, and when it eventually tried to shift to digital, it was too late, and the company couldn't compete with the new entrants in the digital space.

Nokia: Nokia was once the leader in mobile phones. However, it failed to innovate its business model with the advent of smartphones. Despite having the technology, Nokia stuck with its successful feature phone business model, missing the shift in the consumer preference to smartphones. When Nokia finally entered the smartphone market, it was too late, and it couldn't catch up with the likes of Apple and Samsung.

In conclusion, business model innovation is a powerful strategy that companies can use to gain a competitive advantage or even disrupt entire industries. However, it requires a deep understanding of the evolving needs of customers and a willingness to take risks and challenge the status quo. As the examples illustrate, success in business model innovation can lead to significant rewards, but failure can be devastating.

Components of a Business Model and Business Model Canvas

The components of a business model can vary, but most models include the following elements:

Value Proposition: What unique value does the company promise to deliver to the customer?

Revenue Model: How does the company earn its revenue?

Market Opportunity: What are the company's target markets, and how big are these markets?

Operational Model: What are the key activities, resources and partners that are necessary to deliver the value proposition?

Customer Segments and Channels: Who are the company's customers, and how does it reach them?

The right business model can act as a powerful strategic tool, providing a strong foundation for a company to thrive, regardless of market conditions. It can foster innovation, drive growth and provide a clear vision that aligns the entire organization.

To visualize this concept, consider the 'Business Model Canvas', a widely used template that covers the nine key elements of a successful business model:

Key Partners
Key Activities
Key Resources
Value Propositions
Customer Relationships
Channels
Customer Segments
Cost Structure
Revenue Streams

The **Business Model Canvas** is a strategic management template used for developing new business models and for documenting existing ones. It was initially proposed by Swiss business theorist Alexander Osterwalder. (https://www.strategyzer.com/library/the-business-model-canvas)

The Business Model Canvas

Key Partners	Key Activities	Value Propositions	Customer Relationships	Customer Segments
	Key Resources		Channels	
Cost Structure		Revenue Streams		

(Source: www.strategyzer.com)

Key Learnings

Understanding the Importance of Business Models

Business models play a crucial role in determining a company's success. A business model is not merely a financial plan but a comprehensive framework that defines how a company creates, delivers and captures value. It encapsulates the value proposition for customers, the revenue mechanisms and the strategic elements that differentiate a business in the marketplace. The examples of Netflix and Jayaashree Industries illustrate how innovative business models can emerge from identifying and addressing specific customer needs or market gaps.

Traditional Business Models

Traditional business models have their own inherent strengths and weaknesses. The Manufacturer business model, exemplified by Tata Motors and Ford, offers control over production and quality but requires significant capital investment. The Distributor business model, as seen with Redington India and Ingram Micro, leverages economies of scale but faces logistical challenges. Retailers like Reliance Retail and Walmart benefit from direct consumer interaction but must manage inventory and competition. The Franchise model, used by BlueStone and McDonald's, allows for rapid expansion but requires strict control over brand standards. Contract Manufacturing, Licensing, Razor-Blade, Leasing and Bundling models each present unique opportunities and challenges, from cost reduction and risk mitigation to customer loyalty and recurring revenue.

Modern Business Models

The advent of digital technologies and changing consumer behaviours have given rise to several new business models. The

Platform Business Model, used by companies like Ola and Flipkart, leverages network effects to create value but requires significant initial investment. Aggregators like Urban Company and Practo consolidate services to enhance the user experience but face the challenge of maintaining a large user base. On-demand models, such as Swiggy and Urban Company (formerly known as UrbanClap), meet the need for immediacy but must manage fluctuating demand. The Subscription-based model, used by Hotstar and FreshToHome, ensures predictable revenue but struggles with customer retention. The D2C model, exemplified by Lenskart and Mamaearth, offers higher profit margins but demands substantial investment in marketing and logistics. The Creator Economy, C2C, Freemium, Crowdsourcing and SuperApp models each bring unique dynamics to the business landscape, focusing on individual entrepreneurship, community engagement and integrated services.

Hybrid Business Models

Hybrid business models combine elements of traditional and new-age models to create tailored solutions that address specific market needs. Examples include Lenskart and Warby Parker's combination of D2C with physical retail, Flipkart's marketplace plus private label approach, and Nykaa's integration of D2C with retail operations. These hybrids benefit from the strengths of multiple models, such as enhanced customer reach and higher profit margins, but also face challenges related to logistics, brand management and potential conflicts between business operations.

Business Model Innovation

Business model innovation is essential for maintaining competitiveness and addressing evolving market demands.

Successful examples like Reliance Jio and Zerodha demonstrate how disruptive business models can transform entire industries. Conversely, the failures of Kodak and Nokia illustrate the risks of failing to adapt to market changes. Business model innovation involves rethinking how a company creates, delivers and captures value, often requiring significant risk-taking and a willingness to challenge the status quo.

Components of a Business Model

A comprehensive business model includes several key components: the value proposition, revenue model, market opportunity, operational model and customer segments and channels. The Business Model Canvas, developed by Alexander Osterwalder, is a widely used template that encapsulates these elements and serves as a strategic management tool for developing and documenting business models. This framework helps businesses visualize and align their strategies with market conditions and customer needs, fostering innovation and growth.

The landscape of business models is vast and ever evolving. From traditional models that have formed the bedrock of commerce for centuries to innovative new-age models that leverage digital technologies, each approach offers unique advantages and challenges. Understanding these models is crucial for businesses looking to navigate the complexities of the modern market and achieve sustainable growth.

As we progress through the subsequent chapters, we will delve deeper into specific models, exploring their nuances, implementation strategies and the ways they can be leveraged to master the new-age business models and thrive in the digital era.

2
Traditional Businesses Versus New-Age Businesses

In the contemporary business landscape, understanding the differences between pipeline and Platform Business Models is crucial for entrepreneurs and managers. These two models represent distinct approaches to building and scaling businesses in various industries.

Pipeline Business Model

A Pipeline Business Model follows a traditional linear approach to value creation. In this model, value is produced through a sequence of steps that transform raw materials or inputs into finished products or services, which are then delivered to the customer. The Pipeline Business Model has been the dominant approach to business for centuries and is still widely used today. The focus is on achieving economies of scale through mass production and distribution, with the goal of driving down costs and maximizing profits. The Pipeline model is based on supply-side economies of scale, where firms achieve market power by controlling resources, increasing efficiency and fending off challenges from competitors.

Here's a diagram illustrating the linear nature of the Pipeline business:

Pipeline Business - Value flows linearly along the value chain

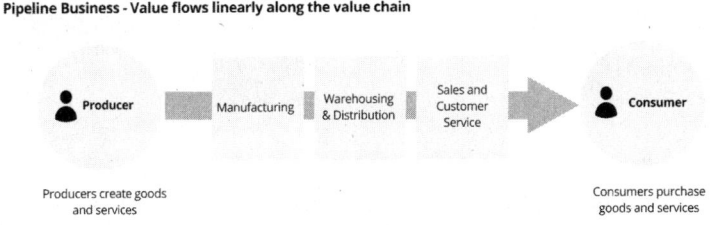

Producer — Manufacturing — Warehousing & Distribution — Sales and Customer Service — Consumer

Producers create goods and services

Consumers purchase goods and services

Platform Business Model

The Platform Business Model is a relatively new approach to creating and delivering value in today's digital economy. Unlike the Pipeline Business Model, which focuses on delivering a product or service through a linear sequence of activities, the Platform Business Model creates value by facilitating interactions and transactions between multiple groups, such as producers, consumers and partners. This is made possible through a multisided platform that connects these groups and enables them to exchange value in various forms, such as goods, services, data or even social connections. The platform acts as a mediator, a matchmaker and a value creator, enabling participants to find each other, transact with ease and derive additional value from the interactions. The Platform Business Model is particularly effective in industries that are information-intensive, network-dependent and characterized by fragmented supply and demand.

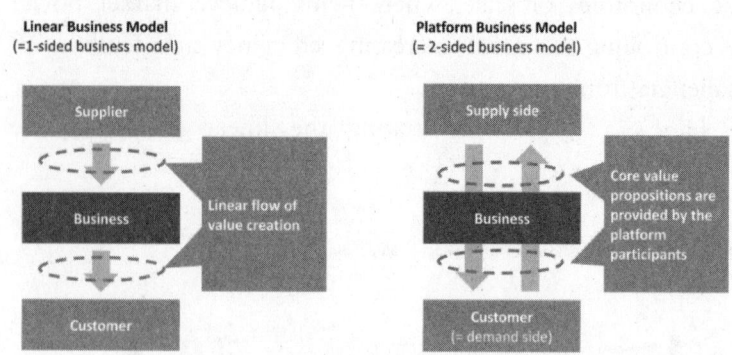

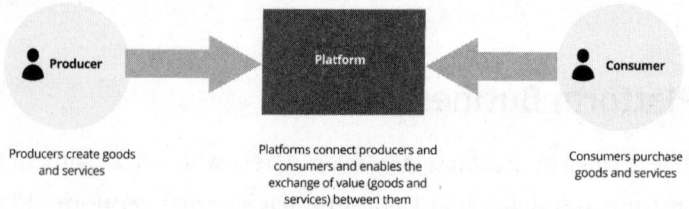

Key Features of Pipeline and Platform Business Models

This table highlights the key features of both Pipeline and Platform Business Models, including their value proposition, key components, revenue model, cost structure, customer relationship management, competition, innovation, ownership, value creation, growth, value maximization and assets.

Feature	Pipeline Business Model	Platform Business Model
Value Proposition	Efficient production and distribution of goods or services	Facilitating interactions and transactions between producers, consumers and partners
Key Components	Linear value chain	Multisided platform connecting producers, consumers and partners
Revenue Model	Sale of products or services	Commission, subscription, advertising or other fees based on platform usage
Cost Structure	Fixed costs, economies of scale	Variable costs, cost of platform development and maintenance
Customer Relationship Management	One-way relationship with customers	Two-way relationship with customers, leveraging data and personalization
Competition	Competition based on quality, price and efficiency	Competition based on network effects, data-driven insights and user experiences
Innovation	Incremental improvements to production and distribution processes	Continuous innovation driven by user feedback, third-party developers and data insights
Ownership	Emphasis on ownership of physical assets and intellectual property	Emphasis on access to shared resources and collaboration
Value Creation	Focuses on delivering a product or service through a linear sequence of activities.	Creates value by facilitating interactions between multiple groups
Growth	More focused on growth via mergers and acquisitions	Grows by creating attractive offerings that draw the attention of partners
Value Maximization	Seeks to maximize the lifetime value of individual customers.	Seeks to maximize the total value of an expanding ecosystem in a circular, iterative, feedback-driven process
Assets	Chief assets are physical resources and capital..	Chief assets are information and interactions, which together are also the source of the value they create and their competitive advantage
Examples	Asian Paints, Tata Motors, HDFC Bank	Flipkart, Amazon, Facebook, OYO, Ola

Key Differences between Pipeline and Platform Business Models

Linear value chain vs complex relationship between producer, customer and platform

A Pipeline Business Model, often referred to as a traditional linear business model, operates in a straightforward way. The value chain flows in one direction: from the producer to the customer. For example, a car manufacturing company like Tata Motors follows a pipeline model where it produces cars and sells those cars to dealers, who then sell to customers.

On the other hand, a Platform Business Model involves a complex relationship between the producer, the customer and the platform. Value is created through the interactions facilitated by the platform. Airbnb is a good example of a platform model. It does not own properties; instead, it provides a platform for hosts (producers) to connect with guests (customers). The value is co-created and shared among all participants.

Single role vs multiple roles and co-creation

In a pipeline model, the roles are clearly defined and separated. The producer creates the product or service, and the customer consumes it. For instance, a fast-food chain like McDonald's produces food that customers buy and consume.

Platform models, however, blur these roles, leading to co-creation of value. On platforms like YouTube, a user can be both a producer (creating and uploading videos) and a consumer (watching others' videos). This fluidity of roles allows for greater interaction and value creation.

Gatekeepers vs open access

Pipeline models often have gatekeepers who control access to goods or services. In traditional publishing, for example, publishing houses decide which books reach the market.

Conversely, platform models tend to promote open access. With self-publishing platforms like Amazon Kindle Direct Publishing, any author can publish their book and reach a global audience, bypassing the traditional gatekeepers.

Standardization vs customization

Pipeline businesses usually rely on standardization for efficiency and scalability. A clothing brand like Zara, for instance, produces standardized sizes and designs for mass markets.

Platform businesses, though, often thrive on customization. Etsy, a marketplace for handmade goods, allows sellers to offer customized products tailored to individual buyers' needs and preferences.

Ownership vs access

In a pipeline model, the focus is on ownership. When you buy a book from a bricks-and-mortar bookshop, you own that physical copy.

Platform models, however, emphasize access over ownership. Consider Spotify, a music streaming platform. Users do not own the music they listen to; instead, they pay for access to a vast library of songs. This model caters to the modern 'sharing economy,' where users value access to diverse resources over owning a limited number of assets.

Drivers of Growth for Pipeline and Platform Business

Drivers of Growth for Pipeline Business Models

Economies of scale

- Pipeline Business Models benefit from economies of scale, allowing them to produce goods or services at a lower cost as they increase production. This can lead to increased profits and competitiveness. This is the traditional 'Supply Side Economies of Scale' that creates strong growth for companies.
- For example, car manufacturers like Maruti and Tata Motors benefit from economies of scale, allowing them to produce cars more efficiently and cost-effectively. Their overhead costs and fixed infrastructure costs get distributed over larger volumes.

Cost advantages

- Pipeline businesses can often achieve cost advantages by optimizing their supply chain and production processes. By minimizing costs, businesses can improve their profitability and offer competitive pricing to customers.
- For example, Walmart is known for its efficient supply chain management, enabling the retail giant to offer low prices to its customers.

Supply chain efficiencies

- Pipeline businesses can also benefit from supply chain efficiencies, reducing lead times and increasing reliability. This can lead to improved customer satisfaction and a competitive advantage.
- For example, Dell's D2C model allows the company to manage its supply chain more efficiently, reducing costs and improving customer satisfaction.

Drivers of Growth for Platform Business Models
Network effects

- Platform Business Models benefit from network effects, where the value of the platform increases as more users join. This can lead to a self-reinforcing cycle of growth and increased market power.
- For example, social media platforms like Facebook and Twitter leverage network effects to create a large user base, increasing the value of their platform.
- This leads to 'Demand Economies of Scale', unique to platform businesses. We will discuss this in detail.

Data-driven insights

- Platform businesses can leverage data to gain insights into customer behaviour and preferences. This can lead to improved user experiences and more targeted marketing efforts. The huge amount of data generated and captured from browsing history, past purchases, cancellations, shopping cart abandonment, content consumption and user journeys can be mined to improve user experience, ensure better conversions and more business for the platform participants.
- For example, Amazon uses data to personalize product recommendations and optimize its supply chain, improving customer satisfaction and profitability. BigBasket uses the data on past purchase and consumption patterns to stock their stores to optimal levels. This is especially important for perishables like fruits and vegetables. The BigBasket website showcases the products most likely to be required, based on past history, to ensure a better user experience.

Platform openness

- Platform businesses can benefit from platform openness, allowing third-party developers to build on their platform and expand its capabilities. This can lead to increased innovation and a larger ecosystem of users and providers.
- For example, Apple's App Store allows third-party developers to create and sell apps, expanding the capabilities of Apple's platform and creating new opportunities for developers and users.

Demand Economies of Scale in Platform Business

Demand economies of scale refers to the phenomenon where the value of a Platform Business Model increases as the number of users and customers grows. As the platform attracts more users, the value of the network grows, making the platform more attractive to new users, creating a virtuous cycle of growth.

One example of demand economies of scale is seen in ride-hailing platforms like Uber and Ola. As more drivers and riders use the platform, the network becomes more valuable, allowing for faster pickups, more efficient routing and lower prices. This increased value attracts even more users to the platform, further increasing its value. The drivers, too, earn more money due to less idle time, faster pickups and more business, thereby attracting more drivers. The 'virtuous cycle' continues.

Urban Company is a platform that connects customers with service providers for a variety of services at home, such as beauty treatments, cleaning, plumbing, carpentry and appliance repair. As more customers join the platform and book services, the demand for service providers increases, creating a virtuous cycle of growth. As more service providers join the platform to meet the growing demand, the platform becomes more valuable to customers, leading to even greater demand.

This increased demand benefits service providers on the platform in several ways. First, they have access to a larger customer base, leading to more work opportunities and less idle time. Second, with more service providers on the platform, the competition among them leads to more competitive pricing. Even with lower prices, service providers can earn more money due to the increased volume of work. This, in turn, attracts even more service providers to join the platform.

For customers, the demand economies of scale lead to more options and better service. With more service providers on the platform, customers have access to a wider range of services and can choose from multiple providers in their locality based on ratings, reviews, availability and prices. As the network grows, the platform becomes more valuable to both service providers and customers, creating a positive feedback loop that drives growth and creates value.

Demand economies of scale can be a powerful driver of growth for platform businesses. As the platform attracts more users, it can offer more value, creating a virtuous cycle of growth and increased market power. By leveraging network effects and data-driven insights, platform businesses can maximize the benefits of demand economies of scale, creating more value for both users and providers.

Metrics to Track

Platform Business Models have distinctly different metrics that need to be tracked for monitoring their state. These differ from the usual metrics in Pipeline businesses that are well known and universally practised—such as Inventory Turnover, Gross

Margins, Accounts Receivables, Contribution Margins, Return on Capital Invested, etc.

Liquidity is a crucial metric for measuring the success of a platform. It refers to the ease of buying and selling goods or services without significantly changing the price. Liquidity is determined by the balance between the availability of supply and the utilization of suppliers. As the platform grows, achieving the right balance becomes more complex, as it requires adding the right amount of supply or demand, being able to intervene manually and addressing marketplace incentives that may work against liquidity.

One example of a platform that measures liquidity is Uber. Uber tracks the time it takes for drivers to accept a ride request and the average wait time for passengers. These metrics help Uber determine the balance between the number of drivers and riders and make adjustments accordingly to improve liquidity. Another example is eBay, which measures the time it takes for an item to sell and the number of bidders per listing. eBay uses this data to ensure that there is enough supply to meet demand and to adjust pricing to maintain liquidity.

A third example is Airbnb, which measures host response rates and the number of bookings per listing. This data helps Airbnb ensure that there are enough hosts to meet the demand and that listings are priced competitively. It also allows Airbnb to intervene when necessary to ensure that hosts are responding in a timely manner and that the platform is providing a good user experience. By tracking liquidity metrics, these platforms are able to maintain a healthy marketplace and ensure long-term success.

Interaction Failure Rate: This refers to the percentage of failed interactions between producers and consumers. Examples include the number of failed rides on Uber or the number of failed bookings on Airbnb.

Engagement Rate: This refers to the percentage of active users on the platform. Examples include the number of daily active users on Facebook or the number of monthly active users on LinkedIn.

Match Quality: This refers to the success rate of matching the needs of users and producers. Examples include the click-through rate on Google search results or the success rate of matching drivers with riders on Uber.

Churn Rate: This refers to the percentage of users who stop using the platform over a certain period. Examples include the number of users who cancel their subscription on Netflix or the number of riders who switch to a competitor of Ola.

Conversion Rate: This refers to the percentage of visitors who take a desired action on the platform. Examples include the number of users who make a purchase on Amazon after searching for a product and viewing the details or the number of viewers who subscribe to a channel on YouTube after watching an episode.

Retention Rate: This refers to the percentage of users who continue to use the platform over time. Examples include the number of subscribers who renew their subscription on Spotify or the number of hosts who continue to list their properties on Airbnb or the number of customers who purchased at least once in the second month at Flipkart.

Customer Lifetime Value: This refers to the estimated value of a customer over their entire lifetime on the platform. Examples include the revenue or the gross margins generated by a customer on Amazon or the commission earned from a driver on Uber.

Net Promoter Score: This refers to the percentage of users who are likely to recommend the platform to others. Examples include the percentage of users who rate their experience with Apple Music as 'highly likely' to recommend or the percentage of riders who rate their experience with Ola as 'promoters'.

Customer Acquisition Cost: This refers to the cost of acquiring a new customer on the platform. Examples include the marketing expenses to acquire a new user on Facebook or the referral bonus to attract new drivers on Uber. Total marketing expenses spent on digital marketing campaigns divided by the number of customers who buy the product.

User-generated content: This metric measures the amount and quality of content that users contribute to the platform, such as reviews, ratings and recommendations. User-generated content can enhance the platform's value proposition and drive engagement. For example, Yelp tracks user-generated content to ensure that its platform remains a trusted source of information for local businesses and consumers.

Negative Network Effects: This is an important challenge for Platform Business Models.

Negative network effects refer to a phenomenon where the value of a platform decreases as more participants join. In other words, as the platform grows, it becomes less valuable to each individual user. Negative network effects can occur for a variety of reasons, such as overcrowding, spam, poor user experience or lack of trust among users. Negative network effects can be especially damaging for platform businesses, as they can result in a loss of users, decreased revenue and ultimately, failure of the business model. One example of negative network effects is seen in social media platforms, where the prevalence of fake news, misinformation and hate speech can drive away users who no longer trust the platform.

Another example of negative network effects can be seen in ride-hailing platforms, where too many drivers on the platform can lead to reduced earnings for each individual driver, resulting in a loss of interest and participation. Negative network effects can also be seen in online marketplaces, where the sheer number of sellers can lead to overcrowding and a lack of differentiation between products, ultimately driving away potential buyers.

Dating apps avoid negative network effects by enforcing community guidelines and ensuring the safety of their users. These apps provide features such as report and block options, which allow users to report any inappropriate behaviour. The app then takes appropriate action, which may include banning the user. Dating apps also use machine learning algorithms to detect and prevent fake profiles and bots, ensuring that the user experience is authentic. Finally, dating apps ensure that user privacy is protected by providing features such as anonymous browsing and the option to hide personal information. These features help avoid negative network effects by creating a safe and positive user experience.

Negative network effects can pose a serious threat to the success of platform businesses, as they can lead to a loss of users, reduced revenue and ultimately, failure of the business model. By taking steps to maintain high levels of trust and quality, improving user experience, and investing in strong governance and moderation tools, platform businesses can avoid negative network effects and continue to drive growth and value creation.

Choice of Business Model: Pipeline or Platform?

When comparing pipeline and Platform Business Models, there are advantages and disadvantages to each of the models. Pipeline Business Models are typically better suited for industries with high fixed costs and predictable demand. In contrast, Platform Business Models are better suited for industries with high variability and uncertainty. Platform businesses are also more agile and adaptable than pipeline businesses, making them better suited for rapid innovation and experimentation. However, platform businesses also face greater regulatory and legal challenges, as well as the risk of network effects that can lead to monopolistic behaviour. Ultimately, the choice between a pipeline or Platform Business Model depends on the specific needs and goals of the business, as well as the industry in which it operates. One of the emerging trends is for traditional pipeline businesses to incorporate key aspects of Platform Business Models to compete and grow better in the face of emerging opportunities and competition.

Real-world Examples:

Pipeline Business Model Examples:

- Ford: Ford follows a traditional Pipeline Business Model, producing standardized cars that are sold through dealerships to customers.
- Walmart: Walmart's retail business relies on a linear supply chain, where products are sourced from suppliers, shipped to distribution centres and sold through physical stores or online channels.
- McDonald's: McDonald's follows a pipeline model, producing standardized food products that are sold through a network of franchisees and company-owned restaurants.

Platform Business Model Examples:

- Airbnb: Airbnb operates a Platform Business Model, connecting hosts (providers) with guests (consumers) to facilitate short-term rentals and experiences.
- Uber: Uber operates a Platform Business Model, connecting riders with drivers to facilitate on-demand transportation.

- Etsy: Etsy operates a Platform Business Model, connecting sellers (makers) with buyers (consumers) to facilitate the sale of handmade and vintage goods.

Hybrid Business Model Examples:

- Amazon: Amazon operates a hybrid business model, combining pipeline elements (such as fulfilment centres and logistics) with platform elements (such as the Amazon Marketplace and Amazon Web Services) to offer a wide range of products and services.
- Apple: Apple operates a hybrid business model, combining pipeline elements (such as manufacturing and supply chain management) with platform elements (such as the App Store and Apple Music) to offer a diverse ecosystem of hardware and software products.
- Netflix: Netflix operates a hybrid business model, combining pipeline elements (such as content production and distribution) with platform elements (such as the recommendation algorithm and user interface) to offer a personalized and seamless streaming experience, incorporating platform model practices in a pipeline business.

How Existing Businesses Can Incorporate Platform Best Practices

Think 'Asset Light'

- Consider how to reduce the number of assets on your balance sheet to increase efficiency

- Example: Instead of holding inventory on their balance sheet, department stores are allowing brands to create subsidiary stores and hold their own inventory

Increase Commission-based Revenue

- Find ways to generate revenue without the costs associated with inventory turnover
- Example: Department stores are earning a percentage of sales from their subsidiary stores instead of relying solely on direct inventory turnover

Encourage Third-party Value Producers to Incentivize Customers to Join the Network

- Leverage third-party producers to help with marketing and customer acquisition costs
- Example: Brands in subsidiary stores carry the inventory risk and have greater incentive to provide sales and marketing to attract customers

Leverage Increased Consumer Demand to Encourage More Producer Participation

- Nurture a virtuous cycle by bringing in more producers to meet rising customer demand
- Example: As more customers engage with subsidiary stores in department stores, additional brands see value in joining the platform

Identify Value to Third Parties Within Your Ecosystem to Create a New Revenue Stream

- Leverage the infrastructure of your business to create new revenue streams

- Example: Department stores partner with third-party financing providers to increase revenue through store-branded credit cards

Incorporating platform best practices can increase efficiency, reduce costs and generate new revenue streams for existing businesses. By asking key questions and considering incremental changes, businesses can find opportunities to implement platform practices and stay competitive in the market.

Traditional Businesses Too Can Incorporate Platform Ideas

In an era where digital transformation is not just a trend but a necessity, many traditional businesses are adopting platform-based strategies to stay relevant and competitive. While these companies have long thrived using conventional business models, the rapid evolution of technology and shifting consumer expectations have compelled them to rethink how they create and deliver value. By embracing the principles of platform businesses—such as data-driven insights, customer collaboration and ecosystems that encourage third-party innovation—traditional firms are opening new avenues for growth and enhanced customer engagement. The following examples illustrate how legacy brands are successfully integrating platform ideas to adapt to the changing business landscape.

Ford's Smart Mobility Initiative

In response to the rise of ride-hailing and car-sharing platforms like Uber and Lyft, Ford has introduced a comprehensive Smart Mobility initiative. This programme integrates platform elements into its traditional vehicle manufacturing business by offering a variety of mobility services. These services include car-sharing and bike-sharing options that work alongside Ford's core vehicle production. One key component of this strategy is the FordPass platform, which enables users to book and pay for parking, schedule vehicle maintenance and access other mobility services. By offering these platform-based solutions, Ford not only broadens its market reach but also positions itself to compete effectively in the rapidly evolving mobility sector.

GE's Predix Platform

GE has embraced platform innovation through the development of Predix, an advanced industrial Internet of Things (IoT) platform. Predix enables customers to collect and analyze data from their industrial machinery, providing data-driven insights that enhance performance and minimize equipment downtime. The platform's open architecture allows third-party developers to build and monetize applications, fostering an ecosystem that encourages continuous innovation and collaboration. By leveraging Predix, GE has transformed its service offerings to be more personalized and efficient, thereby maintaining a competitive edge while delivering greater value to its clients.

Nike's NikePlus Membership

Nike has also incorporated platform thinking into its business model with the NikePlus membership programme. This platform offers members a range of exclusive services, such as personalized training plans, early access to new products, and unique content tailored to individual needs. By creating these personalized experiences, Nike strengthens its relationship with customers and enhances brand loyalty. Additionally, the NikePlus platform gathers valuable data and insights on user preferences and behaviours, enabling more precise marketing strategies and product development. This data-driven approach allows Nike to deliver highly relevant and engaging experiences, transcending traditional product sales.

These examples underscore how traditional companies can successfully integrate platform-based strategies to remain competitive and create new sources of value. By harnessing the power of data, fostering collaboration with customers, and delivering personalized experiences, these legacy businesses are not only staying relevant but are also setting new benchmarks in their respective industries.

3

Key Metrics, Measuring and Tracking New-Age Business Models

The Tale of Doubtnut—A Lesson in Metrics

In 2016, in the bustling world of Indian EdTech start-ups, a start-up called Doubtnut embarked on a journey to transform the way students accessed educational content. With a unique proposition leveraging machine learning (ML) to offer instant solutions to science and maths problems, Doubtnut targeted the needs of millions of students, particularly in India's Tier II and Tier III cities.

Doubtnut's journey in the tech world was akin to a fairy tale. In just three years, the start-up experienced a surge in popularity, peaking at around 1.1 million daily active users by the end of 2019. Its app downloads on Google's Play Store soared past 2.7 million, painting a picture of a company on the precipice of monumental success. These impressive figures—the so-called 'vanity metrics'—caught the eye of big investors. The company successfully raised over $50 million, and everything seemed to be going in the right direction.

One of Doubtnut's critical differentiators was its largely free model, a stark contrast to other major EdTech platforms like Byju's, Unacademy and Vedantu, which offered limited free content. This approach brought a deluge of students to Doubtnut's platform. However, this free service model, while excellent for user acquisition, presented a significant challenge: monetization.

In 2019, the platform, which had relied solely on ad revenue for the first three years, introduced subscription plans. Despite their affordability, Doubtnut faced an uphill battle in converting its free users to paid subscribers. The platform was perceived as a supplementary educational tool rather than a primary resource. This perception problem was a critical issue: Doubtnut offered exceptional value, but in a market where students and parents were already investing in other platforms or local tuition, Doubtnut's offering was seen as an additional and non-essential expense.

Doubtnut's reliance on vanity metrics like app downloads and daily active users, while initially helpful in attracting investors and raising capital, eventually became its Achilles heel. The company's struggle to monetize its offerings effectively became apparent. After seven years and an investment of Rs 800 crore, the company had only about Rs 20 crore in revenue, a stark indicator that despite having a great product, there was a lack of a robust business strategy focused on monetization.

As Doubtnut continued to grapple with these challenges, the situation became more complex. The company's initial strategy, which prioritized user growth over monetization, began to backfire. In the absence of significant new content and product development, user engagement began to wane. The once rapidly growing page views began to drop, and the company found itself with limited resources to innovate or attract new users.

Ultimately, Doubtnut's journey led to an acquisition by coaching chain Allen at just $10 million—a figure that starkly contrasted with its initial high valuation expectations of $100 million to $120 million and far below the $50 million it had raised as capital. This outcome was a sobering reminder of the critical importance of focusing on the right metrics—those that not only track growth and popularity but also align closely with sustainable revenue generation and business model viability.

It underscores the importance of balancing user acquisition and engagement with robust monetization strategies. In the race to scale and grow, companies must carefully choose and prioritize metrics that truly reflect business health and potential for long-term success.

Metrics are the lifeblood of any company's decision-making process. They are quantifiable measures that businesses use to track, monitor and assess the efficiency and success of their operations, strategies and overall performance. These figures not only provide a snapshot of current conditions but also chart a company's progress over time. By setting and analysing specific metrics, companies can make informed decisions, allocate resources wisely, and set targets for future growth. From financial health to customer satisfaction, metrics serve as a navigational tool, helping steer the company towards its goals and alerting it to any adjustments needed to stay on course.

Transitioning from Traditional to New-age Business Metrics

In the rapidly evolving business landscape, a notable shift has occurred from traditional metrics, which focused primarily on financial performance and operational efficiency, to modern metrics that emphasize customer experience, digital engagement and long-term value creation. Traditional metrics such as Revenue, Profit Margin, Return on Investment (ROI), Market Share and Cost Efficiency have been instrumental in assessing the past and present financial health and operational success of businesses. These metrics, being retrospective, focus on past and current financial periods, making them less adaptable to rapid market changes and primarily effective in stable, traditional markets.

However, the advent of digital technology and changing consumer behaviour has necessitated a different approach. New-age metrics like Contribution Margin (CM1 and CM2), Customer Lifetime Value (CLTV), Activation Rate, Average Revenue Per User (APRU), Daily Active Users (DAU), Monthly Active Users (MAU), Churn Rate, Net Promoter Score (NPS) and Viral Coefficient are gaining prominence. These metrics are more forward-looking and emphasize potential future growth and market dynamics. Unlike traditional metrics, modern metrics are highly adaptable to digital trends and market shifts and are crucial for success in rapidly evolving sectors. They are derived not only from internal data but also from external data sources, including digital footprints and social media analytics. This comprehensive approach to data sourcing allows for a more nuanced understanding of the market. We will discuss some of these metrics, their implication for the business and how not to get carried away by vanity metrics.

Popular Traditional Metrics

Let us look at some traditional metrics.

Metric	What it means	How it is measured	How it is calculated
Revenue Growth Rate	Tracking the increase in revenue over time	Comparison of revenue growth during a specific period	[(Current Revenue - Previous Revenue) / Previous Revenue] x 100
Gross Profit Margin	A measure of income after covering the cost of goods sold	The percentage of revenue remaining after Cost of Goods Sold (COGS)	(Gross Profit / Total Revenue) x 100
Net Profit Margin	The portion of revenue that is actual profit after all expenses are deducted	Percentage of revenue after all costs are considered	(Net Profit / Revenue) x 100
Return on Investment	The profitability ratio of the investments	Profitability per dollar invested	(Net Profit from Investment / Investment Cost) x 100
Cash Flow	The net amount of cash being transferred in and out of a business	Net balance of cash during a period	Total Cash Inflows — Total Cash Outflows
Employee Engagement	The level of alignment that employees have towards their work and company values	Through surveys and average scores of employee responses	Aggregate and average responses from employee engagement surveys
Market Share	The company's portion of total sales in the industry	The company's sales as a percentage of the total market	(Company Sales / Total Market Sales) x 100
Customer Satisfaction	Degree to which customers are happy with the company's products or services	Through tracking customer complaints, feedback, surveys and net promoter score	Scoring systems or percentages from customer feedback tools
Customer Acquisition Cost	The expense of acquiring a new customer	Average expense to convert leads into customers	Total Sales and Marketing Expenses / Number of New Customers Acquired
Customer Lifetime Value	The total worth of a customer over the entire relationship	Total margin or contribution a customer is expected to generate	(Average Purchase Value x Average Purchase Frequency) x Average Customer Lifespan x Margin %

Modern Metrics

Modern business models often use many of these metrics. Additionally, based on the type of business, often many new metrics become important. Here are some of the new metrics that have become popular with new models like Marketplaces, Platforms, Software-as-a-service (SAAS) Businesses and Subscription Businesses.

Lifetime Value (LTV): It represents the total revenue a business can expect from a single customer account throughout their relationship. It is crucial for understanding long-term value creation from customers, guiding strategies on customer retention and profitability.

Customer Acquisition Cost (CAC): This metric quantifies the total cost of acquiring a new customer, including marketing and sales expenses. It is essential for evaluating the effectiveness of marketing strategies and understanding the return on investment in customer acquisition efforts.

Retention Rate: It measures the percentage of customers who continue to use a service over a given time period. It is a vital indicator of customer satisfaction and loyalty, and higher retention rates are often correlated with sustained business success.

Annual Recurring Revenue (ARR): Commonly used in subscription-based models, ARR represents the predictable and recurring revenue components of a business, calculated on an annual basis. It is a key metric for assessing the health and scalability of a subscription model.

Viral Coefficient: This metric indicates the rate at which a product or service is being shared or recommended among users. A higher virality coefficient suggests a greater likelihood of rapid user base expansion through word-of-mouth or social sharing.

Activation Rate: It measures the percentage of users who take a desired action (like signing up, completing a profile or making a first purchase) after engaging with a product or service. It is crucial for understanding the initial user engagement and the effectiveness of onboarding processes.

We will discuss some of these metrics in detail. Based on the stage of the organization and the type of business, the key metrics vary. In addition to traditional metrics and new-age metrics, early-stage start-ups have different metrics to track their evolution.

Early-stage Start-up Metrics: Contribution Margin (CM1 and CM2)

In the very early stages, start-ups are busy trying to establish if there is a viable business opportunity to be pursued. The focus is not on profitability but on determining whether there is a need for the product or service, whether customers will buy the offering, whether the customer is willing to pay for the product/service, what the profit margin potential is and how big the business can become. The answers to these questions are usually captured in the concept known as Product Market Fit or PMF. One of the key metrics that this is measured by is the Contribution Margin.

Contribution Margin: The Start-up Metric for Future Profitability

Let us now look at a typical metric that is often used in the start-up world. Start-ups are not profitable initially; they have to spend a significant amount of money to acquire customers, gather data, understand consumer pain points and their behaviour. To understand start-up health, particularly those in their early stages, the conversation often revolves around metrics that differ significantly from those relating to traditional corporate finance. Among these, the CM stands out, particularly, CM1 and CM2.

CM1: This is the net revenue after subtracting the costs directly associated with producing and delivering a product. It is your gross margin and includes variable costs like materials and labour but excludes marketing expenses.

CM2: When we talk about CM2, we are looking at CM1 after deducting direct marketing costs. This metric reveals the revenue remaining after all variable costs have been accounted for, providing insight into the viability of customer acquisition strategies. Direct marketing costs will normally exclude any brand-building or long-term marketing costs,

The Significance of CM2+:

The term 'CM2+' (or CM2 positive) is pivotal in start-up discussions, as it is a strong indicator that a start-up is on the right track towards profitability and has potentially achieved PMF. Becoming CM2+ means that your incremental revenue is covering the costs of generating that revenue, setting the foundation for sustainable growth.

For instance, a SaaS start-up with an annual net revenue of $30,000, experiencing a 30 per cent year-over-year growth, can anticipate an increase in both fixed and variable costs. However, to ensure profitability, the growth in revenue must outpace the growth of these costs. If the start-up maintains a CM2+ status, it is likely to cover its fixed costs over time, indicating a positive trajectory towards profitability.

Relationship Between CM2+ and PMF:

Achieving CM2+ is often seen as a proxy for PMF. A business with sustained CM2+ status has demonstrated its ability to profit from each customer transaction. This profitability is critical before scaling, as it is an assurance that the core business model is sound. If a start-up is CM2 negative (CM2-), it means that it is losing money on each customer, indicating the need for a fundamental change in strategy before pursuing growth.

While CM1 and CM2 are not standard accounting terms, they are essential for start-ups and investors alike as indicators of a company's financial health and potential for profitability. They serve as proxies for future cash flows, crucial for decision-making in the fast-paced start-up environment.

Let us look at an example with some numbers for a hypothetical start-up.

Contribution Margin Example: StreamFast

Revenue and Costs

- Gross Revenue: $500,000
- Taxes, Cancellations and Returns: $50,000
- Net Revenue (Gross Revenue - Taxes/Returns): $450,000

CM1:

- Costs of Goods Sold (Direct Costs): $150,000 (includes content acquisition, server costs, etc.)
- CM1 (Net Revenue - COGS): $450,000 - $150,000 = $300,000
- StreamFast's CM1 reflects the margin after covering the costs directly tied to service delivery.

CM2:

- Direct Marketing Costs: $100,000 (includes performance marketing, ads, etc.)
- CM2 (CM1 - Direct Marketing Costs): $300,000 - $100,000 = $200,000

CM2 takes into account the costs of acquiring customers and is an indicator of whether the core operations, excluding branding and fixed costs, are profitable.

For StreamFast, achieving CM2+ status would mean that their operations and customer acquisition strategies are efficient enough to not only cover variable costs but also contribute to covering fixed costs and, eventually, leading to profitability.

Growth Stage Start-up Metrics

Beyond the PMF stage, comes the question of whether the business is scalable and can grow into a large profitable business. This would depend on the market size and how much share of the market the company can capture. The profitability will depend upon how much money you can make from each customer (contribution or profits) and how much it costs to acquire the customer. In a typical, consumer start-up, these are captured in metrics such as CAC and LTV. Let's look at these metrics.

LTV delves into the projected profit a business can anticipate from a customer's entire relationship, while CAC quantifies the investment required to attract a new customer. By understanding these metrics, businesses can gain valuable insights into long-term profitability, customer retention strategies and effective resource allocation.

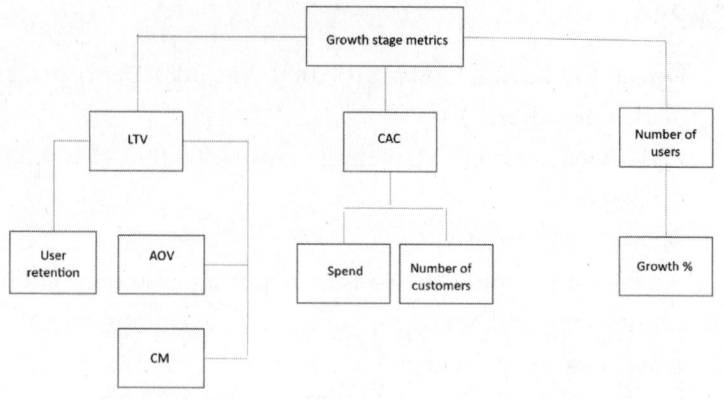

Figure 1: LTV, CAC and User Growth—Key Metrics at
Growth Stage

LTV: Unveiling the Future Value of Customer Relationships

LTV represents a strategic metric that forecasts the profit a business can anticipate from a customer's entire lifespan with the company. This measure is invaluable in understanding the enduring worth of a customer, extending beyond initial transactions. It plays a pivotal role in formulating long-term business strategies and in evaluating the financial significance of customer relationships.

$$\text{LTV} = \text{Average Revenue Per User (ARPU)} \times \text{Customer Lifespan} \times \text{Profit Margin}$$

ARPU is the Total Revenue divided by the Total Number of Customers.

Customer Lifespan denotes the average duration a customer actively engages with a business.

Consider 'HealthFit', a hypothetical fitness app adopting a subscription model:

Average Monthly Subscription: $30

Customer Lifespan: Two years (Twenty-four months)

$$\text{LTV for HealthFit} = \$30 \times 24 = \$720$$

For Swiggy, a renowned food delivery service, let us evaluate the LTV.

Kunal, a regular customer, orders meals worth Rs450 twice weekly and is expected to continue for three years. Swiggy earns a 23 per cent commission on orders.

$$\text{LTV} = \text{Rs}450 \times 312 \text{ orders} \times 23\% = \text{Rs}32,292$$

Adjusting for average delivery costs (Rs20), LTV recalculates to Rs26,052.

This figure represents the potential earnings from a customer over their projected lifespan with Swiggy.

Determinants of LTV

LTV hinges on three core factors: Customer Lifespan, Average Order Value and Profit Margin.

Customer Lifespan: This element is closely tied to customer retention, which inversely correlates with churn. Enhancing customer retention through efficient onboarding, excellent customer service and continuous product improvements can substantially increase LTV.

Average Order Value: Companies can elevate this through strategic upselling and cross-selling.

Profit Margin: This can be improved through optimized sourcing, cost reductions and automation.

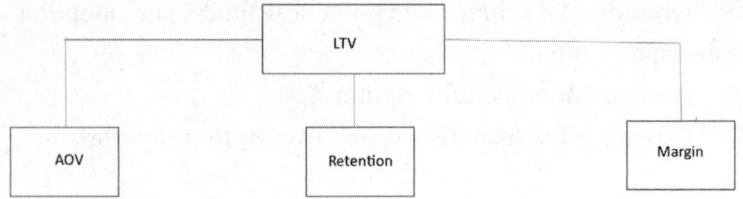

Figure 2: LTV depends on user retention, AOV and the margin on each order

Significance of LTV

Long-term Profitability: LTV is a lens through which businesses can view and understand the long-term profitability of their models, particularly for subscription-based services.

Customer Retention Focus: It underscores the importance of nurturing long-term customer relationships.

Strategic Decision-making: LTV aids in determining investment levels in customer acquisition and retention.

Applying LTV in Business Strategy

Resource Allocation: LTV guides investment decisions in customer acquisition and retention.

Pricing Strategies: It informs pricing to balance profit and customer loyalty.

Customer Segmentation: Identifying high LTV segments leads to more targeted marketing.

Product and Service Development: LTV insights shape product evolution to boost customer satisfaction and retention.

Netflix: With a robust subscription model and strong retention, Netflix's LTV is influenced by continuous content investment.

Starbucks: Known for high customer frequency and loyalty, Starbucks enhances its LTV through its rewards programme.

Apple: Apple's LTV encompasses device sales, app purchases and services, underpinned by its ecosystem approach.

In summary, LTV is a crucial metric for gauging long-term customer value, informing profitability strategies, customer retention tactics and overall business decision-making.

CAC: Measuring the Investment in Growth

CAC quantifies the total expense incurred in attracting a new customer. This metric includes all marketing and sales costs over a defined period, divided by the number of new customers gained. CAC is an essential indicator of marketing strategy effectiveness and spending efficiency in relation to revenue growth.

Calculating CAC:

CAC = Total Sales and Marketing Costs/Number of New Customers during a given period of time

These costs encompass advertising, team salaries, commissions, bonuses and related overheads.

Why CAC Matters

Marketing Spend Efficiency: CAC evaluates the cost-effectiveness of marketing endeavours.

Business Sustainability: An unbalanced CAC to LTV ratio can signal potential growth issues.

Strategic Decision-making: CAC insights are critical for pricing, marketing and customer management strategies.

Examples:

For 'TechGear', a hypothetical e-commerce start-up:

Q1 Marketing and Sales Costs: $100,000

New Customers in Q1: 1000

CAC for TechGear = $100,000/1000 = $100 per customer

Salesforce: Known for its high CAC due to extensive marketing and a direct sales model, Salesforce focuses on achieving a high LTV through long-term contracts and customer stickiness.

Byju's: This EdTech leader employs aggressive marketing and sales tactics, including celebrity endorsements and a large direct sales team. If the company spends Rs100 crore on these marketing activities during the year and acquires 2,00,000 new subscribers during the same period, CAC = Rs5000 per customer.

Flipkart: As a major e-commerce player, Flipkart's customer acquisition involves diverse marketing strategies and partnerships. If the company spends Rs200 crore during the year and it is able to get one million new customers, CAC = Rs2000 per customer.

Evolution of CAC: Companies typically experience higher CAC initially, which gradually decreases as they refine acquisition strategies, optimize spending and improve conversion rates. Different channels exhibit varying CACs.

CAC is a vital metric for assessing marketing and sales effectiveness. Balancing CAC with LTV is key to ensuring sustainable growth and profitability. By optimizing CAC, businesses can enhance strategic decision-making, improve marketing efficiency and boost overall performance.

LTV/CAC Ratio as a Key Metric

The LTV to CAC ratio is a crucial metric that helps businesses understand the relationship between the value they derive from customers and the cost of acquiring

those customers. It is a reflection of the efficiency and effectiveness of a company's marketing and customer relationship strategies.

The ideal LTV/CAC ratio is typically considered to be around 3:1. This means that the lifetime value of a customer should be three times the cost of acquiring them.

Low Ratio (Below 3:1): This often suggests that a company is either over-investing in customer acquisition, acquiring low-value customers or failing to retain customers long enough to recover acquisition costs. It can also indicate inefficient marketing strategies or an overly competitive market environment.

High Ratio (Above 3:1): While this might seem favourable at first, a very high ratio could mean the company is under-spending on acquisition and missing out on growth opportunities. It may also indicate a very loyal customer base but can be a warning sign of market saturation or untapped potential.

A key objective for businesses is to maintain a healthy balance between LTV and CAC. Striving for the ideal LTV/CAC ratio is not just about maximizing immediate profits; it is about sustainable growth and long-term profitability. This balance is indicative of a company's ability to effectively acquire valuable customers while also maintaining healthy margins.

Number of Users and Growth of User Base

The number of users and steady growth are important to build a large, scalable business. Start-ups, particularly those harnessing disruptive and cutting-edge technologies, often face challenges in reaching meaningful scale. Initially, these innovative products or services attract early adopters who demonstrate significant adoption and loyalty. However, the challenge lies in transcending this niche market to gain mass market appeal.

This is referred to as the 'Crossing the Chasm Challenge'. The term refers to the **challenge that technology companies face when trying to transition from serving early adopters of their products to reaching a broader market of mainstream customers. Achieving growth and metrics related to growth are critical for the success of these companies.**

User growth can be achieved through several initiatives such as expanding to new geographies, finding new users with similar needs and moving into adjacencies to address new markets.

Strategies for Achieving User Growth

Expanding to New Geographies:

Companies can grow their user base by entering new geographies.

Ola, an Indian ride-sharing company, expanded its services to Australia, New Zealand and the UK, adapting to local market conditions and regulations.

Netflix's expansion into international markets is a classic example. The company tailored its content and marketing strategies to suit diverse global audiences.

Targeting New User Segments:

Identifying and targeting new user segments with similar needs can lead to significant user growth. This involves understanding different customer profiles and customizing offerings.

Paytm, initially a mobile recharge platform, expanded to cater to a wider audience by offering a variety of services, including payments and shopping.

Spotify's expansion from music streaming to podcasts targeted a broader audience, attracting users beyond just music enthusiasts.

Moving into Adjacent Markets:

Entering adjacent markets is another strategy to address new user needs and expand the user base. This often involves leveraging existing capabilities to offer new products or services.

Reliance Jio, after revolutionizing the telecom sector in India, ventured into e-commerce with JioMart, capitalizing on its vast user base.

Amazon's foray from online bookselling into a broad range of e-commerce and cloud computing services, Amazon Web Services (AWS), exemplifies its effective move into adjacencies.

The Power of Virality Coefficient

The Virality Coefficient stands as a pivotal metric, capturing the essence of growth for products or services via referrals and word of mouth. Predominantly crucial for businesses thriving on network effects like social media platforms and digital apps, this metric adeptly quantifies the influx of new users ushered in by existing ones.

The Virality Coefficient is the heartbeat of user-generated growth, gauging the number of new users each existing user brings aboard. A value surpassing 1 symbolizes exponential growth, showcasing each user as a catalyst for bringing in more than one new user.

$$\text{Virality Coefficient} = (\text{Number of Invitations Sent by Each User}) \times (\text{Conversion Rate of Each Invitation})$$

Illustrative Example: 'AppNet'—A Hypothetical Social Media Phenomenon

1. Initial Assumptions:
   - Every user extends invitations to five friends.
   - A 20 per cent conversion rate, translating to one in five invitations turning into sign-ups.
2. Crunching Numbers: With five invitations and a 20 per cent conversion rate, the Virality Coefficient stands at 1.0.
3. This coefficient signifies a stable, one-to-one user growth.

Dropbox's Virality Triumph

1. Referral Programme Brilliance:
   - Dropbox engineered a referral programme where users, both referrer and referee, gained extra storage space—a straightforward, irresistible proposition.
2. Hypothetical Calculation:
   - Imagining each user recommending the service to ten friends with a 25 per cent conversion rate, we witness a staggering Virality Coefficient of 2.5, indicative of robust exponential growth.
3. Growth Trajectory:
   - This strategy not only caused Dropbox's user base to balloon by 60 per cent but also proved to be a cost-efficient alternative to conventional advertising. The ripple effect of increased usage amplified the platform's value, making it a more integral part of the users' digital lives.

Let us look at another example. Consider a mobile app with 100 users, each referring the app to two people. With a 30 per cent referral conversion rate, the Virality Coefficient lands at 0.6, signalling growth but not of an exponential nature.

Prominent Virality Success Stories:

1. Facebook: Facebook's early ascent was fuelled by its intrinsic virality, with the 2007 introduction of the News Feed escalating user engagement and network expansion.
2. Uber: Uber's 2015 Virality Coefficient, estimated at an impressive 2.4, was propelled by its referral programme which rewarded both riders and drivers.
3. Airbnb: Airbnb's referral programme, offering travel credits for new host and guest referrals, achieved a Virality Coefficient of around 1.53 in 2012, a testament to its effective user growth strategy.

Embracing the Virality Coefficient as a strategic tool can be transformative for today's businesses, especially those banking on network effects and organic user growth. Understanding and harnessing this metric can lead to exponential growth and a dominant market presence, as evidenced by trailblazers like Dropbox, Facebook and Airbnb.

The AARRR Framework: A Comprehensive Metric System

Coined by Dave McClure, founder of 500 Startups and a notable venture capitalist, the AARRR framework, also known as 'Pirate Metrics,' serves as a pivotal model for measuring and optimizing the customer journey. Representing Acquisition, Activation, Retention, Referral and Revenue, this framework is visualized as a funnel through which customers traverse, allowing companies to meticulously measure and refine the flow at each stage.

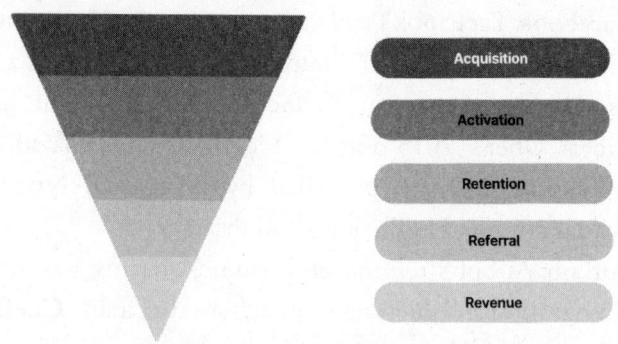

The AARRR Framework

1. Acquisition: The Gateway to Growth
   Definition: Acquisition is the process through which users discover and engage with a product or service. It involves tracking user acquisition from each channel and the associated cost.

   Consider 'FashionStreet', a hypothetical Indian e-commerce entity, leveraging social media advertising, Search Engine Optimization (SEO) and influencer partnerships to draw in visitors.

   If FashionStreet invests Rs1 lakh in social media and attracts 1000 visitors, the cost per acquisition stands at Rs100.

2. Activation: Turning Visitors into Users
   Definition: Activation gauges the extent to which newly acquired users engage meaningfully with the product or service. The focus here is on the percentage of users hitting this activation milestone.

   'TechWiz', a fictional SaaS company, sees activation as users utilizing a key feature within the first week of sign-up.

If 500 out of 1000 new sign-ups actively use a key feature, the activation rate is a noteworthy 50 per cent.

3. Retention: Sustaining User Engagement

Definition: Retention assesses the number of users who continue to utilize the product over time.

'HealthyMeal', an imaginary meal delivery service, tracks repeat orders post the initial purchase. This is quantified as the percentage of repeat customers within a specified time frame. If 300 out of the initial 500 customers reorder within a month, the retention rate is 60 per cent.

4. Referral: Fostering Organic Growth

Definition: Referral measures the extent to which existing customers introduce new users. This involves counting new users gained through such referrals.

'BookBuddy', a hypothetical online book rental platform, rewards its customers for every successful referral. If 100 new users join through a programme, involving 500 existing customers, the referral rate would be 20 per cent.

5. Revenue: The Financial Backbone

Definition: Revenue evaluates the financial contribution from the customer base.

'GadgetZone', a hypothetical retailer in electronics, tracks income from first-time and repeat purchases.
The key here is to calculate total revenue and ARPU.

If GadgetZone earns Rs10 lakh from 1000 customers, ARPU = Rs1000.

Let's look at some examples across each stage of the funnel:

Acquisition Examples:

Flipkart: Utilizes a blend of online and offline marketing, including 'The Big Billion Days,' to secure a broad customer base.

Zomato: Employs targeted digital advertising and partnerships for a significant foothold in the food delivery sector.

Activation Examples:

Byju's: Leverages interactive video lessons and free trials to enhance user engagement and conversion.

Oyo Rooms: Prioritizes an easy booking experience in their app for effective user activation.

Retention Examples:

Swiggy: Retains customers through reliable service and loyalty programmes like Swiggy One, ensuring repeat orders.

Referral Examples:

Paytm: Offers incentives for referrals, significantly enlarging its user base.

Meesho: Grows via referrals on its social commerce platform, especially among home-based entrepreneurs.

Revenue Examples:

Reliance Jio: Disrupted the telecom sector with its initial free services, followed by competitive pricing strategies.

BookMyShow: Generates revenue through ticket sales and partnerships, becoming a premier online ticketing portal.

These instances underscore how companies, cutting across various sectors, have adeptly employed the AARRR framework to nurture and sustain their business growth. Each organization has customized its strategies across the Acquisition, Activation, Retention, Referral and Revenue phases to align with its unique business objectives, demonstrating the framework's versatility and impact on the digital consumer landscape.

Vanity Metrics: Understanding and Navigating the Pitfalls

Vanity metrics are data points or statistics that may look impressive on paper but do not necessarily correlate with the actual health or success of a business. They often give a superficial or exaggerated view of performance. The allure of these metrics lies in their ability to present an overly optimistic picture, making them appealing for businesses to showcase but misleading in terms of decision-making and strategy formulation.

Examples of Vanity Metrics:

1. Page Views: A high number of page views does not necessarily mean increased engagement or conversions.
2. Social Media Followers: A large follower count on social media platforms may not indicate an engaged or relevant audience.
3. Downloads: The number of times an app is downloaded doesn't always reflect active usage or customer satisfaction.
4. Emails Sent: The volume of emails sent in a campaign does not automatically translate into effective communication or sales.

Let us look at a hypothetical company and the challenges it faces when it looks at vanity metrics instead of actionable metrics.

NextGen Media ventured into the digital landscape with a dual focus: operating a social media platform and offering content marketing services. Initially, NextGen Media focused heavily on vanity metrics, which eventually led to strategic missteps and a lack of meaningful growth.

Social Media Platform: The Vanity Metric Trap

NextGen Media's social media platform boasted impressive numbers: millions of followers, likes, shares, comments and impressions. These vanity metrics painted a picture of immense popularity and influence. However, the company failed to focus on actionable metrics like engagement rate, click-through rate, sentiment analysis of comments, social media-generated leads or sales, brand mentions and customer advocacy.

Impact of Ignoring Actionable Metrics:

1. Low User Engagement: Despite high follower counts, the engagement rate was low. Many followers were inactive or uninterested in the content.
2. Ineffective Marketing Campaigns: High impression numbers did not translate into clicks or sales. Marketing campaigns were not tailored to audience interests, leading to poor conversion rates.
3. Misunderstood Audience Sentiment: Without sentiment analysis, NextGen Media was unaware of the growing user discontent, leading to a tarnished brand image.

Content Marketing Services: Overlooking What Matters

In its content marketing wing, NextGen Media focused on metrics like website traffic, page views, unique visitors and download counts. These figures were impressive, but the company neglected actionable metrics such as average time on page, bounce rate, number of returning visitors, lead generation, content-driven sales conversions, customer lifetime value and NPS.

Consequences of Neglecting Actionable Metrics:

1. High Traffic, Low Retention: While the site received a lot of traffic, the high bounce rate and low average time on the page indicated that visitors were not finding the content engaging or relevant.
2. Poor Lead Generation: The focus on the traffic over the leads meant that few visitors were converting into leads or customers.
3. Lack of Customer Insight: Neglecting NPS and customer lifetime value meant that NextGen Media did not understand how its content impacted customer loyalty and value.

As NextGen Media's growth stagnated and the market competition intensified, the leadership realized the need to shift focus from vanity to actionable metrics. They began analysing engagement rates, click-through rates, sentiment analysis, lead generation and customer lifetime value.

By focusing on actionable metrics, NextGen Media was able to:

1. Revamp Social Media Strategy: Tailoring content to user preferences increased engagement and conversion rates.
2. Improve Content Relevance: Analysing time on the page and bounce rates helped them refine content to retain and convert visitors.
3. Enhance Customer Understanding: Through NPS and sentiment analysis, NextGen Media rebuilt its brand image and fostered customer loyalty.

NextGen Media's journey illustrates the pitfalls of over-reliance on vanity metrics and the importance of actionable metrics in driving real business success.

While vanity metrics can be initially appealing due to their positive portrayal of certain aspects of business performance, they often do not offer a realistic or actionable insight into the true state of a company. Realistic metrics, in contrast, provide a more accurate representation of a business's health and are crucial for making informed decisions, driving growth and building sustainable success.

Despite the surge in the popularity of newer metrics, traditional metrics such as revenue growth rate, net profit margin, return on assets (RoA), return on equity (RoE), return on capital employed (RoCE), earnings before interest, taxes and amortization (EBITA), cash flow and market share remain crucial. In the early stages, metrics like Contribution Margin (CM1 and CM2) and Activation Rate are critical for assessing product–market fit and initial customer engagement. As the business grows, the focus gradually shifts to more traditional metrics, aligning with the need to demonstrate profitability and operational efficiency. These metrics provide a solid foundation for assessing a business's financial health and operational success. As companies evolve from early start-up stages, these time-tested metrics gain prominence, complementing the newer metrics to provide a more comprehensive view. Ultimately, metrics like profitability, growth rate, RoCE and RoE are indispensable for assessing long-term success and sustainability.

In summary, a balanced approach to metrics, incorporating both modern and traditional metrics, is critical for a holistic understanding of business performance. Companies must carefully select and prioritize metrics that align with their stage of growth, business model and strategic objectives. By doing so, they can ensure that they have a comprehensive and accurate picture of their performance, enabling informed decision-making and strategic planning. Ultimately, this balanced approach to metrics will pave the way for long-term success and sustainability in the dynamic and ever-evolving business landscape.

Key Takeaways

1. Understand the Difference Between Vanity and Actionable Metrics:
   - Vanity Metrics like app downloads and page views may look impressive but don't necessarily indicate real business health.
   - Actionable Metrics such as CLTV, CAC and Retention Rate provide deeper insights into sustainable growth and profitability.
2. Importance of Monetization:
   - Doubtnut's journey illustrates that focusing on user acquisition without a clear monetization strategy can lead to challenges. Metrics should align with revenue generation and long-term business viability.
3. Transition from Traditional to Modern Metrics:
   - Traditional metrics like Revenue Growth Rate and Net Profit Margin are essential but need to be complemented by modern metrics such as Contribution Margin, Activation Rate and Virality Coefficient.
   - Modern metrics are forward-looking and better suited to dynamic market conditions and digital business models.
4. Early-Stage Focus on Product–Market Fit:
   - For start-ups, metrics like CM1 and CM2 are crucial to evaluate the potential profitability of a product or service before scaling up.

5. Growth Stage Metrics for Scalability:
    *   Metrics such as LTV and CAC become critical at the growth stage to assess the scalability and profitability of the business.
    *   A healthy LTV/CAC ratio (ideally 3:1) indicates efficient customer acquisition and long-term profitability.

6. User Growth and Engagement:
    *   User growth is vital for building a scalable business. Metrics like DAU and MAU help track user engagement and growth.
    *   Strategies for expanding the user base include targeting new geographies, identifying new user segments and moving into adjacent markets.

7. The Power of Virality:
    *   The Virality Coefficient measures how effectively users bring in new users, indicating potential for exponential growth.
    *   A Virality Coefficient greater than 1.0 suggests that each user is driving more than one additional user, leading to rapid growth.

8. The AARRR Framework:
    *   The AARRR (Acquisition, Activation, Retention, Referral, Revenue) framework provides a comprehensive approach to measure and optimize the customer journey.
    *   Each stage of the funnel must be tracked and optimized to ensure overall business success.

9. Balancing Modern and Traditional Metrics:
    *   Despite the emphasis on modern metrics, traditional metrics remain crucial for assessing financial health and operational efficiency.

- A balanced approach that incorporates both sets of metrics provides a holistic view of business performance, ensuring informed decision-making and strategic planning.

10. Long-term Success and Sustainability:
   - Companies must carefully select and prioritize metrics that align with their growth stage, business model and strategic objectives.
   - This balanced approach ensures a comprehensive understanding of performance, paving the way for long-term success and sustainability in a dynamic business landscape.

4

Platforms and Marketplaces

Imagine that you are walking through the bustling streets of an ancient marketplace—a vibrant centre of commerce that has been the heartbeat of civilizations for centuries. From the grand bazaars of Istanbul to the lively streets of vintage Delhi's Chandni Chowk, marketplaces have always been more than just places of commerce; they have been the epicentres of cultural exchange, innovation and social interaction.

The sprawling Grand Bazaar of Istanbul—known as one of the world's first shopping malls—has been a bustling centre of trade since the fifteenth century, offering everything from spices to intricate carpets. India, with its rich history, is home to various traditional markets like Mumbai's Crawford Market and the vibrant Devaraja Market in Mysore, each with its unique offerings and vibrant atmosphere.

Markets were social hubs where people interacted, exchanged news and built relationships—a human touch that often sealed deals through social interactions. The sensory experience of these markets—the sights, sounds and smells—created an ambience that is hard to replicate in the digital world. Transactions were often based on negotiation and trust, with repeat customers and familiar faces forming the backbone of the business.

Fast-forward to the twenty-first century, and the concept of marketplaces has evolved dramatically with the advent of digital technology. While the essence of trading remains, the platforms have been transformed.

Today's digital platforms like Amazon and Alibaba have taken the concept of marketplaces to a global scale, connecting buyers and sellers from different corners of the world. The digital revolution has brought unparalleled convenience and efficiency, making shopping a seamless experience. Unlike traditional marketplaces, digital platforms leverage data analytics to offer personalized shopping experiences.

Home-grown platforms like Flipkart and Meesho have brought the convenience of online shopping to millions, revolutionizing the Indian retail landscape.

Platforms like Zomato for food delivery and OYO for hospitality are examples of how digital marketplaces have diversified to cater to specific sectors.

Introduction to Marketplaces
What is a marketplace?

A marketplace is a platform that connects demand, often referred to as buyers, and supply, often referred to as sellers, to facilitate a transaction. Marketplaces don't own their own inventory, and their role ranges from discovery and matching, transaction enablement and dispute resolution.

Marketplaces exist across verticals and use cases. Some prominent examples of marketplaces include:

- E-commerce marketplaces like eBay, Amazon and Etsy that connect buyers and sellers of products.
- Services platforms like Uber, Ola and Airbnb that match service providers like drivers or property owners with consumers who are looking for rides or a place to stay.
- App stores like the iOS App Store and Google Play Store that connect app developers and users.
- Recruitment sites like Naukri.com, Monster and Indeed that bring together job seekers and employers.
- Social media platforms like Facebook, LinkedIn and Twitter that bring together content creators, content consumers and advertisers.

What all these brands have in common is that they are facilitating a connection between two sides of a market. The demand side is looking for a product or service, the supply side is offering the product or service and the marketplace is creating value by facilitating the demand–supply relationship.

Why Marketplaces Are So Powerful

So what makes a marketplace such a compelling business model? There are three key things that differentiate a marketplace from other business models—scalability, network effects and capital efficiency.

- **Scalability**: Because marketplaces are simply facilitating transactions between third parties, without any inventory or supply chain constraints, they can scale very quickly with limited incremental costs. For instance, if a marketplace like

Uber Eats wanted to expand their restaurant home delivery from 100 to 500 restaurants, they would only have to invest in acquiring the suppliers and product updates so buyers could transact with these new restaurants.

- **Network Effects**: Once a minimum scale is reached, marketplaces experience a virtuous cycle called network effects. As more sellers join a marketplace, there is more variety and availability, making it more attractive to buyers. As a result, more buyers join the marketplace and these buyers transact more often. As more buyers join the marketplace, it becomes more attractive to sellers because there is more demand and more business for them. Marketplaces experience exponential growth with very little additional investment in growing the buyer or seller side of the marketplace.

- **Capital Efficiency**: Because marketplaces don't need to invest in building up their inventory, they can start and operate with very low upfront investment. This low barrier to entry not only makes it easier to build a marketplace, as compared to other types of businesses, it also makes it easier to adapt to changing market needs.

Consider an e-commerce company like Bombay Shaving Company starting up. To become operational, they will need to set up manufacturing, a supply chain to deliver, an online platform to sell, and manage the logistics of home delivery and returns. All this requires significant capital, time and human resources. On the other hand, an e-commerce marketplace like Etsy requires a website, relationships with sellers and, in some cases, the logistics to deliver products to buyers' homes.

Types of Marketplaces

There are a few different variations/flavours of marketplaces, based on the role they play in the transaction, and the types of demand and supply they serve.

Transaction vs Platform Marketplaces

Transaction-based Marketplaces: Some marketplaces are involved in facilitating the transaction between suppliers and buyers. They make it easier for demand and supply to exchange money and play a fiduciary role in the transaction. Often, the marketplace can be held accountable by the demand side if the transaction isn't fulfilled as promised.

For example, Amazon, Filpkart and Alibaba all facilitate transactions between sellers who make products and buyers who are purchasing products. If a buyer isn't happy with the service, they request Amazon for a return, and Amazon ensures that the buyer's issues are resolved.

Platform marketplaces: Yet other marketplaces help supply and demand find each other but are not involved in the process of making the transaction. They often enable the supply side to improve their merchandise and market their offerings but are not responsible for ensuring effective delivery of the service.

A good example of this model is the home services marketplace, Thumbtack. On Thumbtack, homeowners (demand) can find service providers like plumbers, cleaners and contractors. Demand and supply can message each other on the platform, negotiate their own rates and timings for the service. The actual payment is done offline, and not through the platform.

Some marketplaces make a transition from being a discovery platform to a transactional marketplace.

Another example is Zomato, which started off as a restaurant discovery platform, connecting restaurants with customers. Customers could browse menus and read reviews, but the actual transaction of purchasing food/ordering delivery would happen on a different platform or in-person.

In 2015, about six to seven years after its inception, Zomato introduced restaurant pickup/delivery. In this way, it grew from being a discovery platform to a transactional marketplace, enabling the demand and supply side to complete a transaction on the platform.

Business and Consumer Marketplaces

Marketplaces can be divided into three categories, based on who the demand and supply sides on the platform are—business-to-business (B2B), business-to-consumer (B2C) and peer-to-peer (P2P) marketplaces.

	B2B	P2P	D2C
Demand	• Business	• Consumer	• Business
Supply	• Business	• Consumer	• Consumer
Key Features	• Platform capabilities to manage complex transactions. • Enabling trust establishment and dispute resolution.	• Vetting and transaction controls • Discovery and curation. • Payment and fulfillment.	• Streamlined, friction-free transactions. • High-quality buyer experience.
Examples	Alibaba.com FAIRE	Etsy craigslist Quikr	Uber Eats Flipkart

B2B marketplaces

B2B marketplace platforms enable businesses to sell products and services to other businesses. These platforms have revolutionized traditional B2B commerce, offering opportunities for businesses to streamline their operations, expand reach and innovate in procurement and sales processes.

B2B platforms cater to the needs of business entities, from small enterprises to large corporations. Unlike B2C, B2B transactions often involve bulk orders and long-term contracts. Sales processes on B2B platforms are typically longer and more complex, involving multiple decision-makers.

For instance, Alibaba's B2B platform connects suppliers with buyers globally, facilitating bulk product transactions across diverse industries.

In India, IndiaMART is an online B2B marketplace that connects corporate buyers with suppliers across product categories like industrial machinery and building supplies, among others.

In addition to the horizontal marketplaces that cater across sectors, there are several sector-specific B2B platforms. Industrial Goods and Services Platforms, focusing on the supply chain and procurement processes for industrial goods, and IT and Technology Services marketplaces, specializing in IT solutions and technology services procurement, are some examples.

JSW One MSME is an example of a sector-specific marketplace, focusing on the needs of Micro, Small and Medium Enterprises (MSMEs) within the industrial and construction sectors in India. It enables MSMEs to expand their reach by building a strong network of vendors, suppliers and buyers. The platform is designed to facilitate the transformation of MSMEs with minimal cost and investment, providing them with access to a range of building materials and resources.

Characteristics of B2B marketplaces

- **Platform Capabilities to Manage Complex Transactions:** Typically, B2B transactions tend to have a lot of complexities around pricing, custom order requirements and integrations with the buyers' and sellers' enterprise systems (like ERPs). B2B marketplaces that are facilitating online transactions need to have the platform capabilities to handle these complexities.

- **Enabling Trust Establishment and Dispute Resolution:** B2B transactions often take place over multiple face-to-face interactions and discussions with multiple stakeholders. This enables them to establish trust before entering into high-value transactions. B2B marketplaces need to deliver a similar level of trust when facilitating transactions between businesses—by providing adequate information about the products and services being offered, offering fair dispute resolution systems and facilitating secure payments.

In India, the B2B marketplace sector has experienced a significant transformation, driven by greater adoption of smartphones and the need for more efficient supply chain systems. B2B marketplaces in India are streamlining supply chains, enabling small and medium enterprises to reach customers across geographic boundaries as well as to cut costs by reducing the number of intermediaries between them and the customers.

For instance, IndiaMART operates as a platform where suppliers can list their products and buyers can browse and contact suppliers for business transactions. The company earns a revenue primarily through subscription fees from sellers who wish to have greater visibility and premium features on the platform. It has grown to host millions of buyers and suppliers, encompassing a vast range of product categories. Catering to a vast and diverse market, the company has tailored its services to meet the specific needs of different industries and business sizes.

IndiaMART has been particularly instrumental in empowering small and medium enterprises (SMEs) in India, providing them with a platform to expand their reach and compete on a larger scale. The platform's success has had a significant impact on the Indian B2B market, encouraging digital adoption and contributing to the growth of e-commerce in the business sector.

Another B2B marketplace is ShopKirana, an innovative start-up based in Indore. ShopKirana facilitates a direct connection between small retailers, commonly known as 'Kirana Stores', and an array of brands and suppliers. Established in 2015, ShopKirana has quickly risen to prominence in the Indian B2B marketplace, distinguishing itself as a crucial intermediary between retailers and brands.

The company's business model is unique and asset-light, focusing on a zero-inventory approach. Instead of holding stock, ShopKirana acts as a purchasing entity and a multi-brand distributor for retailers. Upon receiving orders from retailers, ShopKirana coordinates with the respective brands. The products are then promptly delivered to ShopKirana's warehouse and dispatched to retailers, usually within three to four hours of the order being received. This expedited process ensures timely deliveries, aiding retailers in maintaining optimal inventory levels and reducing the need for large storage spaces. It effectively shortens the demand–supply turnaround time, eliminates multiple intermediaries and provides the necessary operational expertise and technology. This set-up enables retailers to stay competitive in a rapidly evolving market. The platform also gathers critical data on popular brands, usage patterns and order frequencies, further refining the supply chain's efficiency.

ShopKirana has successfully expanded its operations to several Indian cities, with a strategic focus on increasing its retail network in Tier II regions and beyond.

P2P Marketplaces

In P2P marketplaces, individuals act as both the demand and supply sides of the marketplace. Individuals can trade products and services with each other, bypassing the need for a business intermediary. This model effectively decentralizes commerce and eliminates the premium that is typically charged by intermediaries.

Globally, P2P platforms have seen significant growth, with eBay being one of the oldest and most well-known platforms. eBay offers a wide variety of items from both individuals and businesses and uses an auction-based format. Other notable global P2P platforms include Etsy, known for handmade and vintage items, and Taobao, a leading platform in China. Facebook Marketplace and Craigslist are also significant players, with the former leveraging social media to facilitate transactions and the latter focusing on local communities.

Quikr is an Indian online marketplace and classified advertising company, based in Bengaluru, India. Founded in 2008 by Pranay Chulet, Quikr has listings in over 1000 cities in India and in categories such as mobile phones, household goods, cars, real estate, jobs, services and education. The platform operates on a simple classified listing model, serving as a conduit for buyers and sellers to connect online.

Quikr operates a matchmaking business model where sellers post advertisements for their products for free on the platform, and buyers view these ads and buy the products of their choice directly from the seller. The company generates its revenue from the development and operations of the Internet and mobile transactions. Businesses can promote their products or services on Quikr by posting ads for them. Unlike newspapers, there is no space restriction on ads placed on Quikr. Multiple images can also be uploaded, alongside detailed written descriptions.

Quikr has over ten categories and 170 subcategories, with the most popular being mobile phones and electronics, real estate, cars and bikes. The platform has a feature called Quikr Nxt, which offers instant messaging to seamlessly connect buyers and sellers as per their convenience. Users can choose to make their listing 'private' by hiding their mobile number and using the Quikr Nxt chat feature to connect with buyers.

There are three key characteristics of successful P2P marketplaces.

- **Vetting and Transaction Controls**: Because there are individuals on both sides of the transaction, the role of the marketplace is to guarantee trust and security. This is done by vetting demand and supply and offering transaction controls.
  - For instance, each time somebody buys a product on eBay, the money goes into an escrow owned by eBay and is only released once the product has been delivered.
- **Discovery and Curation:** Marketplaces enable individuals to discover the most relevant products for them from a large range of sellers across geographical and other boundaries.
- **Payment and Fulfilment:** One of the biggest barriers standing in the way of individuals being able to transact with each other is the giving and receiving of payments, ensuring smooth shipping and returns and dispute resolution. P2P

marketplaces play a critical role in enabling a smooth transaction between the two parties.

B2C Marketplaces

B2C marketplaces are where businesses sell products or services directly to consumers. Amazon and Flipkart are examples of B2C marketplaces, where business owners can sell their products to buyers.

B2C marketplaces have revolutionized the world of commerce and services, bringing enterprises and individuals who would not have otherwise discovered each other closer together. This has led to a significant increase in the availability and diversity of products and services for the average consumer.

B2C marketplaces serve a few critical roles for both sides of the transaction:

- **Streamlined Transactions**: These B2C marketplaces often provide integrated services like payment processing, logistics, delivery and customer support. This means that they need to have excellent logistics and supply chain processes to provide a better experience, as compared to purchasing directly from the sellers.
- **High-quality Buyer Experience**: The most successful platforms like Amazon and Uber Eats provide a standardized and high-quality buyer experience across a wide range of sellers, which increases buyer retention and satisfaction. This is particularly important for B2C marketplaces because the barrier to entry is low for new marketplaces, and the switching cost for buyers is also low, creating a highly competitive environment for these players.

Take the food delivery industry, for instance. In the US alone, there are over six options for buyers—Uber Eats, Grubhub, Doordash, Postmates, Seamless and Caviar. Buyers will choose the platform that offers them the most seamless experience, the best prices and the assortment of sellers that they want to purchase from.

In India, Flipkart is one of the most successful B2C platforms. Starting as an online bookstore, Flipkart today offers a plethora of products from electronics to fashion and home goods. As an early entrant into the Indian e-commerce space, Flipkart was able to capture significant market share and customer loyalty early on.

Over time, their sharp focus on delivering a seamless, user-friendly experience, both through their product interface and through reliable logistics, has helped them retain a market share of 48 per cent as of FY23, serving 400 million customers across India.

Monetization Strategy

Marketplaces have revolutionized the way businesses operate, creating a digital bridge between demand and supply across industries. A critical aspect of their success lies in their ability to generate revenue through various streams, ensuring sustainability and growth. This section explores the diverse revenue models adopted by platforms and marketplaces, illustrated with examples from global and Indian contexts.

	Commission-based Pricing	Listing Fee Model	Lead Fee Model	Subscription Pricing	Ad-based Pricing
Description	• Marketplace takes a percentage of the transaction value as a fee.	• Marketplace charges flat fee to list on the marketplace.	• Marketplace charges flat fee to list on the marketplace.	• Marketplace charges a subscription fee to either demand or supply.	• Marketplace allows sellers to advertise on their platform, and charges a fee for impressions and leads received by the seller.
Benefits and Drawbacks	• Effectively aligns seller and marketplace incentives. • High risk of disintermediation to avoid transaction fees.	• Simple model, creating upfront revenue for marketplace irrespective of transaction value. • Does not align supply value to marketplace incentives.	• Aligns the marketplace's revenue with value for sellers. • Cost-prohibitive for sellers who have low lead conversion fee.	• Steady stream of recurring revenue for marketplace. • Challenging to deliver ongoing value to justify the subscription costs.	• Revenue stream for platforms that don't facilitate transactions. • Reduces options available for demand.
Examples	SWIGGY	Etsy	Thumbtack	Angi	Etsy OLX

Commission-based pricing: Marketplaces that facilitate transactions take a percentage of the transaction value as a fee. Marketplaces like Airbnb, Uber and Swiggy all operate on a commission-based pricing model.

Commission-based pricing is effective at aligning the incentives of sellers and the marketplace, as sellers only pay when they make a sale. However, it requires a high enough volume of transactions and transaction value to be successful. Commission-based models are also most likely to suffer from the risk of disintermediation, where supply and demand match through the marketplace but take the transaction offline to avoid transaction fees.

Most commission-based pricing marketplaces are characterized by two key metrics—Gross Merchandise Value (GMV) and Take Rate. GMV is the total value of all transactions happening on the platform, while the Take Rate is the percentage commission that the marketplace charges.

Listing Fee Model: Some marketplaces charge a listing fee. The seller pays a flat fee for listing their products or services on the marketplace. For example, Etsy charges a $0.20 fee for each item listed on the platform.

While this is a relatively simple model, and creates revenue upfront, this model doesn't align value to sellers with the marketplaces' incentives.

Lead Fee Model: Some marketplaces charge for the leads that sellers receive through the marketplace. For instance, Thumbtack, the home services marketplace, charges service providers for each warm lead they get through the platform.

While this model aligns the marketplace's revenue with value for sellers, it might be cost-prohibitive for sellers who have a low lead conversion rate.

Subscription pricing: Some marketplaces charge a subscription fee to either demand or supply for the services that the marketplace offers. While this helps the marketplace have a steady stream of recurring revenue, it can be challenging to deliver value at a high frequency to justify the subscription costs.

Angi, a home services marketplace, offers a premium offering to homeowners (demand) to get access to discounted home services (supply) in exchange for an annual subscription fee.

Platforms like Zomato Pro offer subscription-based models providing discounts and perks, enhancing customer loyalty and predictable revenue.

Ad-based pricing: Some marketplaces allow sellers to advertise on their platform and charge a fee for the impressions and leads that sellers receive. Etsy, Amazon and X all offer this option to sellers. These advertised sellers show up as 'sponsored' on the listing page.

Amazon, Etsy and OLX generate revenue by offering advertising space to businesses and premium listing options to sellers.

While this model creates a revenue stream for platforms that are not facilitating transactions, it disincentivizes supply side players who can't afford to pay for advertising, reducing the options available for demand.

Growth Strategy

One of the things that makes a marketplace an incredibly powerful business model is the flywheel of network effects. As the marketplace acquires more supply, it increases the options available for demand—leading to greater acquisition and retention of demand. As more demand joins the platform, supply gets more business through the platform—increasing the acquisition and retention of supply.

When the flywheel of network effects is in play, the marketplace experiences exponential growth with little to no additional investment in acquisition, making the business highly defensible.

When a marketplace is experiencing this flywheel, they are said to have reached 'optimal liquidity'. Liquidity is a measure of how effectively the marketplace is enabling transactions between buyers and sellers. If a marketplace is 'liquid' or has reached 'optimal liquidity', it means that buyers can reliably and efficiently find what they are looking for, measured by the 'search-to-fill rate', and sellers can reliably and efficiently sell what they want to sell, measured by the 'supply utilization rate'.

For instance, Uber's demand liquidity would be measured as the percentage of ride requests that result in successful rides. Supply liquidity is measured as the percentage of drivers that are working 100 per cent of the time.

So how does a marketplace get to optimal liquidity? First, the marketplace needs to build a critical mass of demand so that it can attract enough supply to get the flywheel going. Second, it needs to build up a critical mass of supply so that the demand it has attracted can be served. And third, it needs to enable effective matching between demand and supply.

Building Critical Mass of Demand and Supply

- **Pick a Narrow Market:** To get to a critical mass of demand and supply, many marketplaces start with a very small and concentrated market. This enables them to make their acquisition efforts more customized and specific, instead of spreading themselves thin across multiple markets.

- **Build Single-player Features:** Some marketplaces grow initial demand or supply by building single-player features that don't rely on the network effects. This enables them to build up to a critical mass of demand or supply early. For example, OpenTable first launched a reservation system for restaurants to manage their own bookings. Once they gained sufficient regional density of restaurants, they opened up the consumer side of the marketplace

- **Offer Incentives:** While incentives are not a long-term strategy, they can be a powerful way for marketplaces to get to the critical mass of supply or demand.
  - For example, Uber offered guaranteed earnings or bonuses to new drivers to encourage them to join the platform.

- **Leverage Existing Communities:** Identify and engage with pre-existing communities of supply or demand.
  - For example, Etsy engaged the crafting and handmade goods community in its early days. Many of these artisans were already selling locally at craft fairs or on their own websites. By providing them an online platform to reach a wider audience, Etsy was able to tap into this existing community of makers to build its initial supply base.

Effective Matching Between Demand and Supply

- **Personalized Recommendations:** By using Artificial Intellegnce/Machine Learning or AI/ML algorithms and data about user preferences and behaviours, marketplaces can recommend the products or services that the demand is most likely to value.
  - For instance, Amazon's recommendation engine analyses user behaviour, purchase history and item relationships to suggest the right products to demand.

- **Dynamic Pricing:** Some transactional marketplaces adjust prices in real time to better balance supply based on variations in demand.
  - Uber uses dynamic pricing to ensure driver availability during peak times by increasing fares.
- **Search and Filtering Capabilities:** Most marketplaces use search and filtering functionality to help demand efficiently find what they're looking for.
  - Airbnb enables users to filter listings by location, price, amenities and more, facilitating the discovery of ideal accommodations.
- **Ratings and Reviews:** A huge part of a marketplace's value proposition is building trust between demand and supply. Ratings and review systems enable discovery.
  - Yelp and Zomato's review systems are a core part of what helps restaurant-goers find the right restaurants.
- **Real-time Matching Algorithms:**
  - Ride-sharing platforms like Uber and Lyft use sophisticated algorithms to match drivers with passengers in real time, optimizing routes and reducing waiting times. This not only improves the user experience but also increases the number of rides per driver, contributing to the platform's liquidity.

On-demand Business

- An on-demand business leverages technology to provide immediate access to products or services, fulfilling consumer needs with speed, if possible, instantly. This requires a flexible workforce (gig workers), and the ability to manage demand and supply very well.
- The categories of on-demand include ride-hailing apps like Uber and Ola, food delivery apps like Swiggy and Zomato,

quick commerce companies like BB Now (Bigbasket), Instamart (Swiggy), Blinkit (Zomato) and Zepto. Home services is another category, with Urban Company in India and Taskrabbit in the US as examples.

- Over-the-top (OTT) streaming services, like Netflix, Amazon Prime, Jio Cinema, etc., have overtaken traditional cable TV.

- Three key requirements for an on-demand business to be successful include technology, demand prediction and building a flexible and responsive supply of products and people. Other than the streaming services, all other categories tend to use a large population of gig workers or flexible staffing paid on a transaction basis.

- The technology requirements for on-demand business include app/web access for easy discovery and ordering by customers. Using past behaviour to serve the best options to customers, curating the mostly likely products/services that they may wish to consume, helps with customer experience, as well as increasing the customer lifetime revenue. Identifying the service provider, tracking their movements and providing real-time updates to customers on the status of delivery is essential too. Using Internet of Things (IoT) tracking on the products being shipped can also help with real-time logistics updates. On-demand businesses tend to use AI/ML to help predict customer tastes and demands so that they can match the supply appropriately. Strong systems for customer support, using AI bots as well as humans, is essential as the expected turnaround time for delivery is very limited.

- A flexible workforce is another key requirement for on-demand businesses, e.g., food delivery businesses like Swiggy and Zomato have created a new cadre of delivery personnel. We see them congregating near popular eateries. Grocery delivery organizations such as Blinkit and Zepto are likely to need pickers and packers in the 'dark store' as well as delivery personnel for the last mile. The supply of the workforce needs to be flexible and adapt to the changing demand patterns. Offering suitable training, fair compensation and incentive structures, support by way of insurance and healthcare and community feeling are essential for maintaining a workforce that is committed to the business. There has been a lot of debate on whether gig workers should be provided any support beyond the per-visit earnings by the business, as they may work across multiple platforms and no one platform is their primary employer.

- For gig workers, this can be an additional job that they take up during their free hours, a job that provides them with incremental income. They can get substantially higher per-hour compensation during festivals or peak timings, and this can make it a very attractive option. Some on-demand platforms, such as Urban Company, provide a marketplace of skilled workers like beauticians, plumbers, deep cleaners, etc. Typically, such workers are likely to be registered with multiple platforms or even have their own shops and pick up these job requests as additional income-generating options.

Q-commerce (Quick commerce)

- One interesting example of on-demand business is Q-commerce, which has grown meteorically over the last few years. The size of this business is currently estimated to be around $2.8 billion and is expected to continue to grow at 40 to 50 per cent Compounded Annual Growth Rate (CAGR) for the near future. Companies like Swiggy and Zomato, which started with food delivery, have added grocery delivery under Swiggy Instamart and Blinkit respectively, and are seeing a big growth in this segment. Zepto started as a pure play Q-commerce player and has seen good growth in revenue and valuations too. BigBasket, a leading grocery delivery player, added BB Now to provide a solution to this growing demand for instant delivery. These Q-commerce products fulfil product delivery in a time frame of eight to twenty minutes. While cooking, if you realize that you are missing an ingredient, it can be delivered instantly so you can continue cooking.

- When Q-commerce first started, products were picked up from neighbouring stores and delivered. However, the fill rate and margins in this model were not very satisfactory. This led to the setting up of 'dark stores' in the neighbourhood that stocked all the products as per plan but had no customer interface. These stores served as a pick and pack facility, with products stored based on projections of demand in the neighbourhood. As the business picked up momentum, the projections and, consequently, the stocking got better, leading to improved availability and margins. To increase the average order value, the companies added non-food items, including cosmetics, health and wellness products, apparel, small home goods, etc., to their offerings. [1]

Future Trends

Marketplaces and on-demand businesses will continue to evolve rapidly with new technologies and customer preferences shaping this evolution.

---

[1] Bhatnagar, Kushal. 'Unveiling India's Q-Commerce Revolution'. *Redseer*, March 7, 2024, Grocery section, https://redseer.com/newsletters/unveiling-indias-q-commerce-revolution/.

Innovations such as personalized shopping experiences using AI, virtual try-ons with Augmented Reality (AR) and streamlined logistics solutions are shaping the future of B2C e-commerce, enhancing customer engagement and operational efficiency. The B2C market is witnessing trends like the rise of mobile commerce, increased focus on sustainability and the integration of social media for shopping. Platforms such as Instagram have started becoming marketplaces, with individuals and small businesses using the platform to develop reach and offer their merchandise directly to their fans. Voice commerce through the likes of Alexa and Google Home is also picking up momentum.

AI and ML are being used by a number of organizations to improve the demand–supply matching, and to predict customer preferences even as they evolve.

Key Takeaways

1. Evolution of Marketplaces:
   - Historical Significance: Traditional marketplaces, such as the Grand Bazaar of Istanbul and India's Crawford Market, served as social hubs where commerce, cultural exchange and social interaction occurred.
   - Modern Digital Platforms: Digital marketplaces like Amazon, Alibaba, Flipkart and Meesho have revolutionized commerce by connecting buyers and sellers globally, leveraging data analytics for personalized shopping experiences and offering unparalleled convenience and efficiency.
2. Definition and Types of Marketplaces:
   - Marketplaces Overview: Marketplaces are platforms that connect buyers and sellers to facilitate transactions

without owning inventory. Their roles include discovery, matching, transaction enablement and dispute resolution.

- Types of Marketplaces: Examples include e-commerce (Amazon, eBay), services (Uber, Airbnb), app stores (iOS App Store), recruitment sites (Naukri.com) and social media platforms (Facebook, LinkedIn).

3. Powerful Attributes of Marketplaces:
   - Scalability: Marketplaces can quickly scale up with limited incremental costs due to their role as facilitators rather than as owners of inventory.
   - Network Effects: As marketplaces grow, they become more attractive to both buyers and sellers, creating a virtuous cycle of exponential growth.
   - Capital Efficiency: Marketplaces require lower upfront investment compared to traditional businesses, making them adaptable to changing market needs.

4. Variations of Marketplaces:
   - Transaction vs Platform Marketplaces: Transaction marketplaces facilitate and oversee transactions (e.g., Amazon), while platform marketplaces connect supply and demand without being involved in the transaction process (e.g., Thumbtack).
   - Business and Consumer Marketplaces: These include B2B (Alibaba, IndiaMART), P2P (eBay, Quikr) and B2C (Amazon, Flipkart) marketplaces, each catering to different types of buyers and sellers.

5. Monetization Strategies:
   - Commission-based Pricing: Platforms like Airbnb and Uber charge a percentage of the transaction value.
   - Listing Fee Model: Platforms like Etsy charge a fee for listing items.

- Lead Fee Model: Platforms like Thumbtack charge for leads generated.
- Subscription Pricing: Platforms like Zomato Pro offer subscription-based models for discounts and perks.
- Ad-based Pricing: Platforms like Amazon and Etsy generate revenue from advertising space.

6. Growth Strategies:
- Building Critical Mass: Marketplaces achieve optimal liquidity by attracting a critical mass of buyers and sellers, facilitated by incentives, leveraging existing communities and offering single-player features.
- Effective Matching: Marketplaces use personalized recommendations, dynamic pricing, search and filtering capabilities, ratings and reviews, and real-time matching algorithms to enhance the user experience and drive transactions.

7. On-demand Business Models:
- Key Requirements: Success in on-demand businesses, such as ride-hailing (Uber), food delivery (Swiggy) and quick commerce (Zepto), relies on technology, demand prediction and a flexible workforce.
- Technology and Workforce: Essential technologies include apps for easy discovery, AI/ML for demand prediction and IoT for real-time logistics updates. A flexible workforce, often gig workers, is crucial for meeting dynamic demand patterns.

8. Future Trends:
- Technological Innovations: Personalized shopping experiences using AI, AR virtual try-ons and streamlined logistics solutions are shaping the future of marketplaces.

- Integration with Social Media: Platforms like Instagram are evolving into marketplaces, allowing small businesses to reach customers directly.
- Voice Commerce: The rise of voice-assisted shopping through devices like Alexa and Google Home is gaining momentum.
- AI and ML: Continuous advancements in AI/ML are improving demand–supply matching and predicting customer preferences.

Marketplaces and on-demand businesses have transformed traditional commerce by leveraging digital technologies, creating global connections and offering convenience and efficiency. The success of these platforms lies in their scalability, network effects and capital efficiency. As technology evolves, marketplaces will continue to innovate, providing personalized, seamless experiences to meet changing customer expectations. Embracing these trends will be crucial for businesses aiming to thrive in the dynamic digital landscape.

5

'SaaS: The Breadth and Lifeline of Modern Enterprises'

Imagine stepping into a time machine, not to explore the distant past or a future world, but to witness the evolution of how we use and interact with software in our daily work lives. This journey started in the late 1990s and early 2000s, when the idea of accessing powerful software applications without the need for bulky hardware or tedious installations seemed like a distant dream. Businesses, large and small, were tethered to physical servers, cumbersome software packages and a constant cycle of upgrades and maintenance that demanded significant resources, both in terms of time and money.

Now, fast-forward to the present, where the landscape of software distribution has undergone a seismic shift, thanks to the advent of SaaS. This model has democratized access to cutting-edge technology for businesses of all sizes and introduced a level of flexibility and efficiency previously unimaginable. Imagine a small start-up now leveraging the same powerful tools as a Fortune 500 company without the need for a hefty upfront investment or an IT department to manage complex installations and upgrades. The playing field has been levelled, innovation has been unleashed and business transformation has accelerated.

Two pivotal shifts sparked this dramatic transformation. First, the explosion of Internet connectivity and the emergence of cloud computing which together made it possible to deliver software over the Internet with unparalleled speed and reliability. (Cloud computing is a technology that allows businesses and individuals to access and store data, applications and services over the Internet, rather than on local servers or personal devices. This shift to cloud-based solutions offers significant advantages, including scalability, cost-efficiency and flexibility). Second, the rise of Infrastructure-as-a-Service (IaaS) providers like Amazon Web Services, which offered on-demand access to computing resources, further reduced the barriers to entry for software providers.

The SaaS model has reshaped the B2B software industry, bringing to life a new breed of agile, innovative companies that could easily adapt to changing market demands and scale globally. It has also shifted the power dynamics in the vendor–customer relationship, putting the emphasis on customer satisfaction and ongoing value rather than upfront sales and long-term contracts.

Introduction to SaaS

SaaS is a distribution model for software where software applications are hosted by a third-party provider and delivered through the Internet to its end users and customers.

This was in contrast with the predominant model at the time, where a business purchased software as well as the hardware needed to host the applications, and the software had to be installed on specific devices and accessed through those devices.

Most of the maintenance was owned by the customers, and any upgrades required additional contracts with service providers.

Let's understand this with an example from the video conferencing industry.

In the traditional enterprise software model, a customer would enter into a multi-year contract with a service provider like Cisco. They would buy the hardware and software packages and licences, requiring configuration, integration and installation before use.

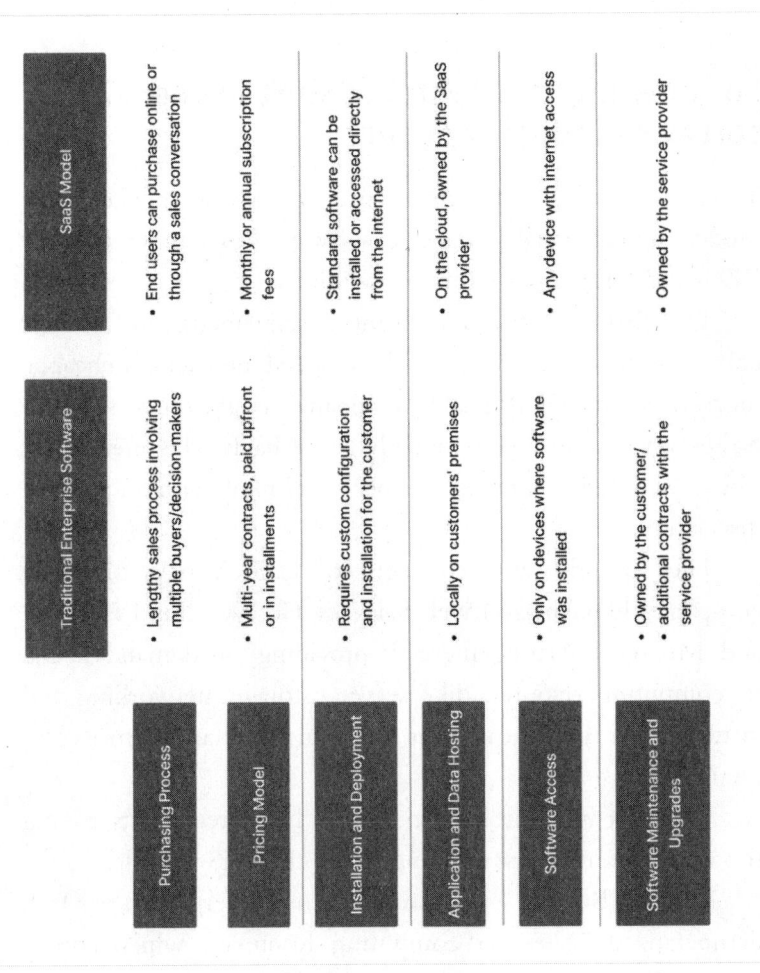

	Traditional Enterprise Software	SaaS Model
Purchasing Process	• Lengthy sales process involving multiple buyers/decision-makers	• End users can purchase online or through a sales conversation
Pricing Model	• Multi-year contracts, paid upfront or in installments	• Monthly or annual subscription fees
Installation and Deployment	• Requires custom configuration and installation for the customer	• Standard software can be installed or accessed directly from the internet
Application and Data Hosting	• Locally on customers' premises	• On the cloud, owned by the SaaS provider
Software Access	• Only on devices where software was installed	• Any device with internet access
Software Maintenance and Upgrades	• Owned by the customer/ additional contracts with the service provider	• Owned by the service provider

In contrast, a SaaS-based provider like Zoom can be purchased, installed and accessed via the Internet for a monthly or annual subscription fee. There is no hardware needed as the application is hosted on the cloud, and any updates or maintenance are handled by Zoom at their end.

So, how did this tectonic shift in the B2B software industry occur?

The foundation for the emergence of SaaS as an alternative model to traditional enterprise software was laid in the late 1990s and early 2000s with two key shifts:

The first was the significant advancements in internet connectivity and broadband. As high-speed internet got cheaper, more widespread and reliable, companies could access software hosted on remote servers quickly and reliably. This meant that software could be delivered 100 per cent online without physical installation.

The second was the advent of IaaS. A new breed of companies like Amazon Web Services, Google Cloud Platform and Microsoft Azure emerged, providing on-demand access to computing resources like servers, storage, networking and virtualization. This meant that companies had an alternative to ownership.

These technological advancements had three effects, paving the way for a new class of companies—the SaaS providers.

Lower Barrier to Entry: The emergence of IaaS democratized access to computing resources, which meant that smaller upstarts could enter the B2B software industry and compete with the incumbent traditional enterprise software players.

Ability to Serve Small–Medium Businesses (SMBs): Since SaaS providers were paying for computing resources based on usage, they could offer services at smaller Annual Contract Values, based on the customer's overall needs. This opened up a new market—small–medium businesses—that had, to date, been unserved or underserved by traditional enterprise software companies.

Ability to Expand Beyond Geographical Constraints: It enabled SaaS providers to offer their applications to any customer worldwide, expanding their total addressable market far beyond geographical borders and opening up a new horizon of the unserved customer base.

Why Did Customers Value SaaS?

From a customer perspective, SaaS provides a desirable alternative to traditional enterprise software. There were three keyways in which it differentiated itself—flexibility, cost and ease of use.

Flexibility: With traditional enterprise software models, customers would have to purchase additional licenses, server capacity and hardware, if they wanted to scale up usage. This required negotiating new contracts through a lengthy sales process.

With SaaS models, customers can scale their services up and down, based on demand and usage, whenever they want. This flexibility and control over their software usage had two benefits.

First, it was a better ROI than traditional models since customers only had to pay for what they were using and could pay more or less based on usage for a given month.

Second, it improved the overall end-user experience. If end users are not happy with the product, they will stop using it, and the customer will downgrade. As a result, the SaaS providers were incentivized to prioritize the end-user experience, and not just the buyer experience as traditional enterprise software incumbents typically did.

Cost Effectiveness: SaaS changed the overall economics of purchasing and using software.

First, the upfront cost of adopting a new software is nearly zero with SaaS. Companies can try products for free or at a low price, especially with the increasing proliferation of freemium and free trial models.

Second, instead of committing to annual contracts, which locked them into a single price for a whole year, monthly subscription models enabled companies to upgrade, downgrade or cancel at any time, reducing the overall cost burden for a given year.

Take Shopify, for example. The upfront cost to start using the product is zero. Later, companies can pay a monthly fee for usage. The amount they pay depends on the services they want. They can seamlessly upgrade from a lower tier to a higher tier with just a credit card swipe, instead of going through lengthy processes.

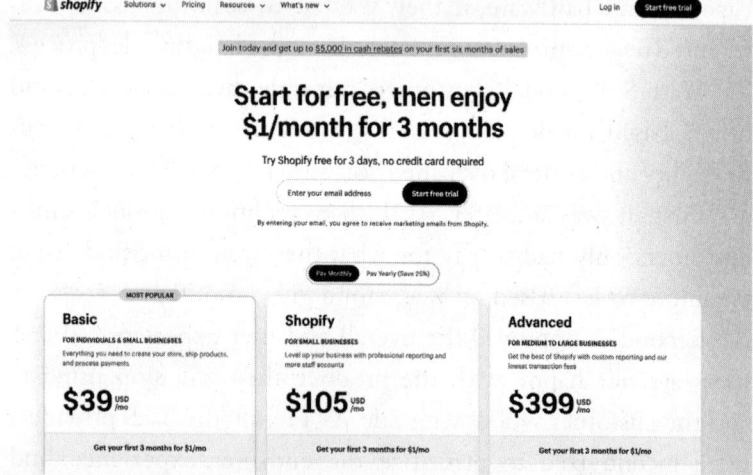

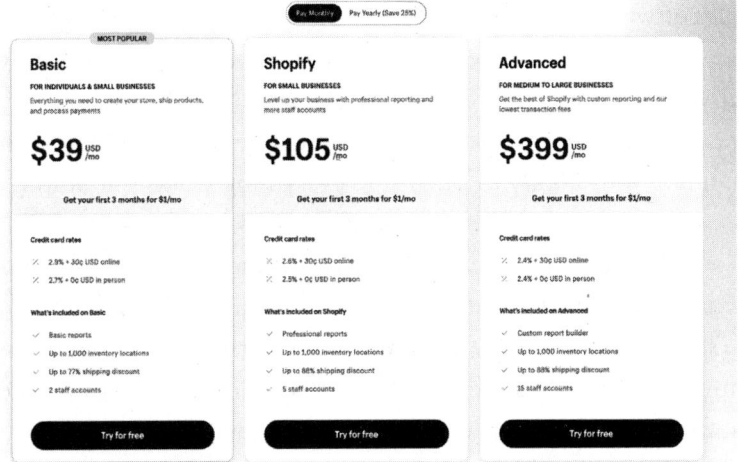

Source: Shopify website

Third, the overall costs were also lower since SaaS providers were a lot more efficient—they didn't have to spend as much on installation, sales and marketing or owning computing resources. They passed these cost savings on to their customers, reducing the total amount customers had to pay for similar services.

Ease of Access, Use and Upgrades:

Because software is deployed over the cloud, customers can access the software through multiple devices and systems—desktop, browser, mobile app, etc.—while traditional alternatives can only be accessed via the system in which the application was installed.

In addition, SaaS providers can seamlessly and continuously update the software with the latest features and security updates. This enables customers to access the most current versions with minimal overhead of installation/deployment and integration.

Think of a music streaming service like Spotify. Imagine you have an extensive music library on your personal computer using old software that must be installed and updated manually. With this setup, you can only listen to your music when you are physically at your computer. If you want to upgrade the software, you may need to download a new version, install it, and sometimes even migrate your library to make sure everything works smoothly.

Now, compare this to Spotify, a SaaS-based service. With Spotify, you can easily access your music library from your smartphone, tablet, desktop or even your car's smart audio system. You don't have to worry about manually updating the app to get new features or security enhancements because the software updates seamlessly in the background. As a result, you always have the latest version without the hassle of complex installations or configuration. This is the ease and flexibility that SaaS brings to software usage.

Again, Zoho made significant updates to their workplace platform in 2021—offering a unified, AI-driven search across the Zoho suite, a centralized dashboard and new collaboration tools. This update was immediately available to all its customers as soon as they launched. In addition, as they made further improvements to each of these features, they would be deployed immediately, unlike traditional enterprise software models where updates would be batched into a new version that customers would have to install proactively.

Salesforce Case Study

Salesforce, now a gold standard in the Customer Relationship Management (CRM) domain, was one of the early pioneers of the SaaS business model.

Founded in 1999 by Marc Benioff, Salesforce's vision was to create CRM software that was hosted entirely on the Internet. This was in stark contrast to the incumbent players like SAP and Oracle, which were hosted on-premises, instead of on the cloud, and required heavy upfront investment to purchase and deploy, with annual contracts that offered flexibility to scale up and down.

Salesforce was also one of the first B2B software companies to offer a monthly subscription pricing model, instead of the annual contracts of incumbents like Oracle's Siebel Systems and SAP.

Traditional CRMs (SAP, Oracle)	Salesforce
On-premise	Cloud-based
Annual contracts	Subscription model
Designed for corporate buyers, not user-friendly	Designed for end users

Salesforce started by targeting small and medium businesses that found its suite of features and price points better aligned with their needs and budgets. These companies, that traditional enterprise software companies did not serve, helped Salesforce establish itself in the CRM software industry, learn about customer needs and refine its product offering enough to target more significant and more established customers.

Over time, Salesforce expanded its product offerings, going beyond customer relationship management to include customer service, marketing automation and analytics. This enabled it to adopt a 'land and expand' strategy to acquire and grow its ARR. Salesforce would acquire a customer with its flagship offering, CRM, and then, over time expand to other use cases that built on top of the data it already had access to, like customer service or marketing messaging.

Key Metrics

Three key metrics are used to measure the health of a SaaS business:

- Net Dollar Retention is a measure of the revenue from a given month that is retained in the following month.

- New Revenue Growth is a measure of revenue brought in by acquiring new customers in a given month.
- LTV:CAC Ratio measures how much value is created by acquiring and serving a customer.

Net Dollar Retention

The net dollar retention (NDR) looks at how much revenue, earned in a given month, is retained in the following month. It provides a holistic view of how well a company is retaining, engaging and growing its customer base.

$$\text{Net Dollar Retention (NDR)} = \frac{\text{Starting Monthly Recurring Revenue} + \text{Expansion Revenue} - \text{Contraction Revenue} - \text{Churned Revenue}}{\text{Starting Monthly Recurring Revenue}} \times 100$$

(*Contraction revenue* refers to the decrease in revenue from existing customers, which can occur if customers downgrade their plans or reduce the number of services they use. *Expansion revenue* is the additional income generated from existing customers through upselling or cross-selling, such as when a customer upgrades to a higher-tier plan or purchases additional features. Finally, *churned revenue* represents the revenue lost when customers cancel their subscriptions or do not renew their services. Together, these components provide a comprehensive view of how a SaaS company is maintaining and growing its revenue base over time.)

The most successful SaaS companies have an NDR of over 100 per cent, which indicates that they are not only retaining revenue, but also growing the revenue from each customer month-over-month. Conversely, companies whose NDR is <100 per cent are losing more revenue month-over-month and will have to significantly increase new customers to grow their overall revenue.

The 2023 median net retention for all SaaS companies was 102 per cent. Some high-performing SaaS companies at IPO had an average net retention rate of 139 per cent.[1] Generally, it is considered if a company's NDR is around 110 per cent, it is in line with the average, and if it is around 120 per cent or more, the company is doing exceptionally well

New Revenue Growth

New customer growth measures how many new customers a SaaS company adds in a given period. New revenue growth measures how much revenue is earned from new customers in a given time.

Net Revenue Growth = Number of new customers × Average revenue per new customer

New revenue growth is an essential indicator of a SaaS product's ability to continue to attract and convert new customers, and its ability to continue to differentiate itself in the market and compete against incumbents and new players in the industry.

LTV:CAC Ratio

The third key metric to evaluate the health of a SaaS company is the LTV:CAC ratio, or the lifetime value of a customer divided by the cost to acquire the customer. The LTV:CAC ratio measures how much value acquiring and serving a customer creates for a business.

---

[1] 2023 SaaS Retention Benchmarks for Private B2B Companies—SaaS Capital

A good LTV:CAC ratio for a SaaS company is typically between 3:1 and 5:1. This means that for each dollar spent to acquire a customer, the company is earning between $3 and $5 through the customer's lifetime.

On the other hand, if the LTV:CAC ratio is below 1, the company will not be able to recover the cost of acquiring the customer through the customer's lifetime.

Understanding the LTV:CAC ratio helps SaaS companies know what kind of customers they should focus on acquiring and retaining, which acquisition channels are most effective in yielding profitable customers and how much to spend on the customer.

LTV is a measure of the total revenue a customer has contributed throughout their lifetime as a customer. There are two ways to calculate it.

LTV = Average Monthly Recurring Revenue per Customer × Customer Lifetime

$$LTV = \frac{\text{Average Monthly Recurring Revenue Per Customer}}{\text{Customer Churn Rate}}$$

CAC measures the cost of acquiring a new customer and is calculated by dividing the total cost of sales and marketing by the number of new customers acquired during the period. Typical acquisition costs include sales personnel salary and commissions, marketing technology and human resource costs, cost of advertising, partnerships and other marketing campaigns.

$$CAC = \frac{\text{Total Sales and Marketing Spend}}{\text{No. of Customers Acquired}}$$

Many SaaS companies and investors also track the payback period on acquisition cost. This is a measure of how long it takes for a company to recover the cost of acquisition.

While exact metrics for SaaS companies are not always publicly available, various industry reports and sources provide indicative estimates to offer a glimpse into the performance and efficiency of these organizations. It is important to note that these figures are subject to variation based on the time period for which they are reported, as the SaaS business environment is dynamic and constantly evolving. For instance, during the pandemic, Customer Acquisition Costs (CAC) were notably lower due to reduced options for customer engagement, but as conditions normalized, CAC increased as companies needed to reinvest in more diversified and expensive acquisition strategies.

To illustrate, Salesforce has an estimated CAC ranging from $4,000 to $12,000, depending on various factors such as sales team costs and marketing expenditures. The company's Lifetime Value (LTV) of a customer varies between $36,000 and $50,000, resulting in an LTV:CAC ratio between 3:1 and 9:1. Salesforce's Net Dollar Retention (NDR) is estimated between 110% and 120%, reflecting strong customer retention and revenue expansion through upselling and cross-selling.

Similarly, HubSpot's CAC is around $10,000, with an LTV estimate of $40,000 to $45,000, yielding an LTV:CAC ratio of approximately 4.5:1. Its NDR falls between 100% and 105%, indicating stable retention with modest growth. Zoom Video Communications is known for its highly efficient acquisition strategies, with a CAC of approximately $1,000 to $1,200 and an impressive LTV of $10,000 to $20,000, giving it an LTV:CAC ratio of 10:1 to 18.5:1. Zoom maintains a strong NDR of around 130%.

Adobe Creative Cloud's figures suggest a CAC range of $3,500 to $5,000 and an LTV between $20,000 and $40,000, translating to an LTV:CAC ratio of 4:1 to 8:1. The company boasts a stable NDR of 120%. Lastly, Shopify, with its e-commerce focus, has a relatively low CAC of $300 to $600 but a higher LTV range of $2,000 to $5,000, giving an LTV:CAC ratio of 5:1 to 10:1. Shopify's NDR varies from 120% to 150%, driven by rapid expansion and increasing customer spend.

These metrics underscore how efficient customer acquisition and strong customer retention can significantly impact the financial health and long-term sustainability of SaaS businesses.

Evolution of SaaS and Its Status Today

Since its first avatar in the early 2000s (Salesforce, founded in 1999, and Netsuite, founded in 1998, being famous examples), SaaS has gone through many waves of evolution to become an $165 billion dollar global industry today. Industries, ranging from technology and finance to manufacturing and retail, have adopted SaaS products to serve their needs across customer relationship management, software development and administrative workflows, such as accounting and human resource management.

There are three pillars of strategy—product strategy, go-to-market strategy and monetization strategy—that make or break a SaaS player. A SaaS company's choices on these three pillars differentiate their ability to acquire and retain customers, become profitable and differentiate themselves from their competition.

Product Strategy

The first axis of evolution was around industry focus. In the early 2000s, most SaaS companies were 'horizontal' players. This meant that their solutions were broadly applicable across industries.

For instance, Salesforce CRM could be used by e-commerce companies, technology companies or the pharmaceutical industry. Similarly, Box, the file storage solution, could be used in education, content or financial services.

As the adoption of SaaS grew across market segments and traditional enterprise software providers like Microsoft and Adobe began offering SaaS solutions, the B2B software industry became more competitive. So new players needed to find a way to differentiate themselves.

On the demand side, as niche industries like life sciences, construction and fintech became more sophisticated and comfortable adopting software solutions, there was an opportunity to serve the unique needs of these industries that incumbent solutions were not adequately serving.

This led to the emergence of more 'vertical' SaaS companies. These providers offer solutions personalized to the needs of specific industries, serving the workflows, compliance and security needs of these industries. For instance, Veeva Systems provides solutions specifically for the life sciences industry, while Mindbody provides scheduling software for the wellness services industry.

This specialization has a few key benefits:

- Lower cost of acquisition: By targeting a particular set of customers in a given industry, the acquisition strategies could be made more focused and offer a higher return on investment.
- For instance, a vertical SaaS company, targeting the pharmaceutical industry, would develop relationships with pharmaceutical companies by participating in trade shows, advertising in journals, joining industry associations, etc.

In contrast, a horizontal SaaS company would be targeting many different industries through lower ROI channels like digital marketing, advertising and sales teams, thereby having a higher acquisition cost per customer.

- Higher revenue retention and expansion: By offering more personalized solutions and support, vertical SaaS companies see higher customer and revenue retention and can expand to adjacent use cases, expanding revenue from each customer.

- Larger market share in niche: With a domain-specific focus, the SaaS provider will have a stronger recall and brand in their industry of choice, and their proactive investment in product development for the industry will help them continue to deepen their penetration of their industry and gain strong dominant market share.

- For instance, a company like Veeva has captured 60 per cent of the pharma CRM market. In contrast, a horizontal CRM provider like Salesforce has about 20 per cent market share.

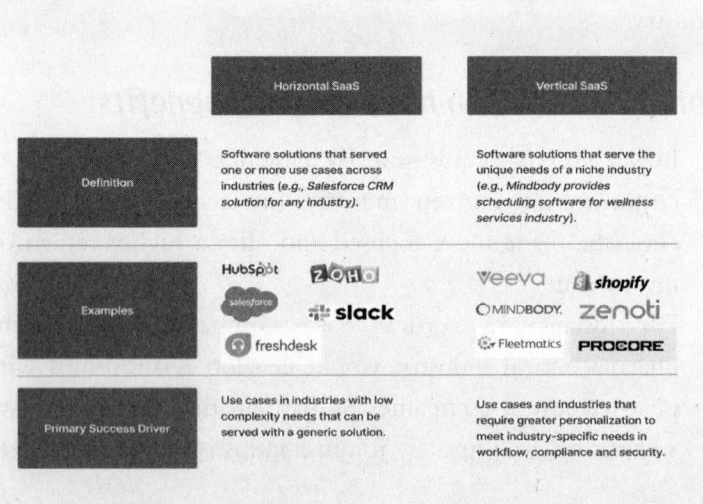

	Horizontal SaaS	Vertical SaaS
Definition	Software solutions that served one or more use cases across industries (e.g., Salesforce CRM solution for any industry).	Software solutions that serve the unique needs of a niche industry (e.g., Mindbody provides scheduling software for wellness services industry).
Examples	HubSpot, ZOHO, salesforce, slack, freshdesk	Veeva, shopify, MINDBODY, zenoti, Fleetmatics, PROCORE
Primary Success Driver	Use cases in industries with low complexity needs that can be served with a generic solution.	Use cases and industries that require greater personalization to meet industry-specific needs in workflow, compliance and security.

Today, horizontal and vertical SaaS providers coexist to serve different use cases and industries.

Horizontal SaaS providers are best suited to serve use cases in industries with low product complexity, and generic solutions satisfy most of the needs. Products like Asana for project management, Slack for communication, Notion for productivity, or Salesforce for CRM are flexible enough to serve varied customer needs.

Vertical SaaS, on the other hand, is better suited for use cases in industries with unique needs in workflow, compliance, security, etc. Vertical SaaS providers can quickly evolve their product offerings to meet the industry's changing needs, and the lower cost of acquisition can be passed on as lower costs to customers.

Go-To-Market (GTM) Strategy

The second major factor that differentiates SaaS companies today is their go-to-market motion. There are three common GTM strategies that SaaS companies adopt—self-serve (or product-led growth), sales-assisted or inside sales and sales-led GTM. The right strategy for a SaaS company depends on their offerings' target market, product complexity and price point.

In the self-serve GTM motion, customers sign up, use and manage the software independently without the involvement of the SaaS provider's sales or support team. In most cases, the acquisition, onboarding and monetization motion are all driven by the product, without any human intervention in any part of the process.

This is called product-led growth (PLG) and has helped companies like Figma that serve prosumers and small–medium businesses scale up quickly and cost-effectively.

A prosumer is a "producer" and a "consumer" both simultaneously. Some common examples of prosumers are tech-savvy users who create their own programmes, videos, memes and other content. They are also often the first adopters of new technologies and services, giving valuable feedback to companies in the process.

- **Zoho**: Zoho is another great example of an Indian SaaS company that uses a PLG strategy to reach a global market. The company offers over 50 business applications, from CRM and finance to HR and analytics. Zoho's products are known for their user-friendly interfaces and easy onboarding, making it simple for users to sign up, explore the features and start using the software with minimal assistance. The freemium model and free trials attract a broad audience, and many users eventually upgrade to paid plans as their needs grow.
- **Chargebee**: Chargebee provides subscription management and billing software and has leveraged a PLG model to reach small and medium-sized businesses. The product is designed to allow users to set up and manage their billing operations independently. Users can start using Chargebee with minimal help, and the product itself drives further engagement and growth. Chargebee has a strong focus on delivering a seamless experience, which has helped the company scale rapidly and serve thousands of customers worldwide.

For PLG companies, acquiring and onboarding customers costs significantly lower than sales-assisted or sales-led GTM as the process is user-friendly with low friction to start and derive initial value.

In addition, usage of the core product supports the acquisition of new users, enabling the product to scale up quickly to a large number of users.

For example, Calendly is a meeting scheduling tool that allows people across and within organizations to find mutually agreeable meeting times. One of the most potent user acquisition modes is through invites. When a user hosts a meeting and invites a non-user to join it, the non-user learns about the product and considers signing up and creating an account, becoming a user and host themselves, further driving growth.

Calendly serves over twenty million users across 1,00,000 client companies at an average annual selling price of <$100. Their product-led growth model enables them to serve their large user base at scale.

As a result, SaaS companies choose the self-serve GTM motion under three conditions:

- When the target market is a **large volume of small, medium businesses or prosumers** with relatively undifferentiated needs, the self-serve motion enables companies to reach many individuals and companies and scale up quickly.
- When the **product is simple and needs configuration**, since all the onboarding is happening through the product, without any human support, this model works best when users can set up and use the product without any assistance.
- When the **average selling price (ASP) is zero or low**. When the ASP is high, the buying decision requires significantly greater consideration and more stakeholders across procurement—company leadership and user teams—and requires some human touchpoints to be completed.

In the sales-assisted or inside sales motion, sales or customer support representatives are involved in the acquisition and onboarding journey, often through remote touchpoints like phone calls, email or video conferencing. The sales process is typically much faster than it is in traditional sales motions, with fewer touchpoints between the customer and the SaaS provider.

For example, HubSpot uses inside sales techniques like phone calls, emails and online demos to reach and sell to target customers. The sales representatives use a consultative sales approach, using quantitative data and qualitative discussions to understand customer needs and personalize the sales process and solutions.

As of 2023, HubSpot has 1,50,000+ customers with an average selling price of around $10,000 USD. This volume and price point enable it to effectively use inside sales techniques to serve its customers' needs, scale up at the right pace and support its cost of acquisition.

With the sales-assisted motion, since there is a human representative, the company can establish a relationship with their customers and assist them in configuring and personalizing the product for their use case and for onboarding users. This helps the customer to use the product most effectively and increase the value delivered. In addition, because many of the sales are happening remotely and with fewer touchpoints than there are in sales-led motion, the cost of acquisition and onboarding is lower than in the sales-led model, and sales cycles are also lower.

As a result, SaaS companies choose the inside sales motion for products with three characteristics:

- The target market is **medium-volume (not large numbers like small enterprises and not small numbers**

of large corporations but in-between these two ends) of midsize companies. A sales-assisted motion is more straightforward than a sales-led motion when it comes to scaling up.

- **When the product is of medium complexity** and requires personalization and onboarding/education for customers to get value from the product.
- **For medium ASP products ($50–100K range).** This is a high enough price point that the buying decision requires some human interfacing but not high enough to support a full-fledged sales process.

The third model of sales-led go-to-market involves a full sales motion where sales representatives have a series of touchpoints with target customers, buyers, decision-makers and influencers.

For instance, SAP, the provider of enterprise resource planning (ERP) software, adopts a sales-led go-to-market strategy for its complex sales cycle.

Workday is another example of a sales-led company. They specialize in HR and financial management software, targeting large organizations like AT&T, Morgan Stanley and Abbott that need customized human capital management solutions. Today, they have about 10,000 customers, with an average selling price of around $500,000–$1 million.

The most significant advantage of the sales-led motion is that it allows the provider to establish a deeper relationship with their customers and understand their unique needs and use cases. This enables them to customize better and personalize the product, educate the user base, and eventually create the path for upselling and cross-selling based on adjacent and emerging needs of the customer.

As a result, SaaS companies choose the sales-led motion in a few situations:

- When the target market is a small volume of **medium and large enterprises**.
- When the **product is highly complex** and requires a lot of configuration and personalization for a customer, and training and onboarding a large user base to ensure that the customer realizes the product's value.
- When the **ASP is high**, it is often up to multimillion dollar annual contracts. This high price point requires deep relationship-building with multiple stakeholders to close the sale. The price point also enables the relatively high cost of acquisition to be supported by a sales-led motion.

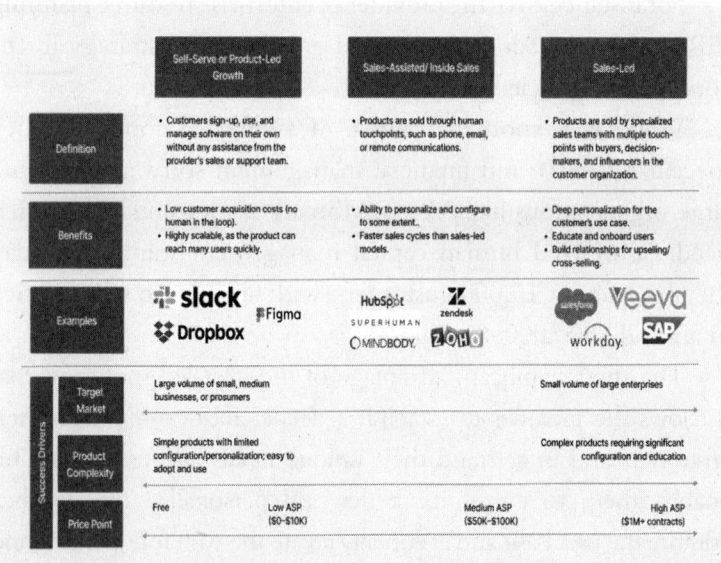

While some SaaS companies use one of these go-to-market motions, increasingly, SaaS companies have a variety of products and/or use cases that target different markets and use different go-to-market motions.

For example, HubSpot has a free version of their CRM to attract individuals and small businesses to start using its platform. In this way, users experience the value of the software, and the acquisition cost for HubSpot is also relatively low.

For small to medium businesses, HubSpot has an inside sales team that engages with leads who have shown interest in the free product or other inbound marketing tools. This inside sales team helps sell slightly larger Annual Contract Values at lower acquisition costs than a full-fledged sales team.

They also target large enterprises with a sales-led approach. Sales staff offer personalized demos, detailed product walk-throughs and personalized solutions to the complex and varying needs of these enterprises.

Monetization and Pricing Strategy

One of the most significant competitive advantages that SaaS companies offer over traditional enterprise software is a pricing model that is more flexible and economical for small and medium businesses. Instead of pricey annual contracts, SaaS companies charge monthly subscription fees and pricing plans that vary based on specific features and functionality that customers want to use.

There are broadly three ways in which SaaS companies charge their customers for the products and services they offer—feature-differentiated pricing, usage-based pricing and value-based pricing.

	Feature-Differentiated Pricing	Usage-Based Pricing	Value-Based Pricing
Definition	• Pricing varies by tier, with each tier offering a set of features and functionality. • Users choose the tier based on the feature set they intend to utilize.	• Price varies based on customer's usage of the product.	• Price varies based on the actual value the product delivers to the customer, like revenue generated or time saved.
Benefits	• Flexibility to pay. • Predictability in the price.	• Strong alignment between cost and usage for customers.	• Strong alignment between cost and value for customers.
Drawbacks	• Not all customers are likely to use all features equally, leading to misalignment between price and value.	• Low predictability in costs. • Usage doesn't always equate to value delivered.	• Challenging to quantitatively estimate the value delivered. • Perceived value varies by customer making it hard to price.
Examples	• Salesforce offers several tiers for CRM product with more advanced set of features.	• AWS employs a usage-based pricing model where customers pay for the computing resources they consume.	• Amplitude charges customers based on the number of users they are tracking on amplitude, or monthly tracked users.

Feature-Differentiated Pricing

With feature-differentiated pricing, the price that users pay varies by tier, with each tier offering a different set of features and functionality. Users choose the tier based on the feature set they intend to utilize.

This model offers customers the flexibility to pay only for the feature sets they are using while also having an understanding of what they will pay in a given month or year.

However, because customers are paying for a predefined set of features, they may not always use all the features. This makes users believe that they are paying for more than they are using.

Take the example of Wistia, a video platform for marketing teams. They offer feature differentiated pricing; they have four tiers, and each tier provides a different set of features. So, for instance, if customers value email integrations, they would choose the Plus plan or above. If they need A/B testing and a custom Call to Action (CTA), the Pro plan would be suitable for them.

A/B Testing: A/B testing, also known as split testing, is a method used to compare two versions of a web page, app or other digital content to determine which one performs better. By showing different versions (A and B) to different segments of users and analysing the results, companies can make data-driven decisions to improve conversion rates, user engagement and overall effectiveness of their digital assets.

CTA: A CTA is a prompt on a website or digital content that encourages users to take a specific action. Common CTAs include buttons or links that say 'Sign Up,' 'Buy Now,' 'Learn More' or 'Subscribe.' Effective CTAs are designed to guide users towards completing a desired task, such as making a purchase, filling out a form or downloading a resource.

While customers benefit from only paying for the feature set most relevant to them, they may only sometimes use all the features included in the tier. If a customer values A/B testing but doesn't plan to use custom CTAs, they would still have to choose the Pro plan.

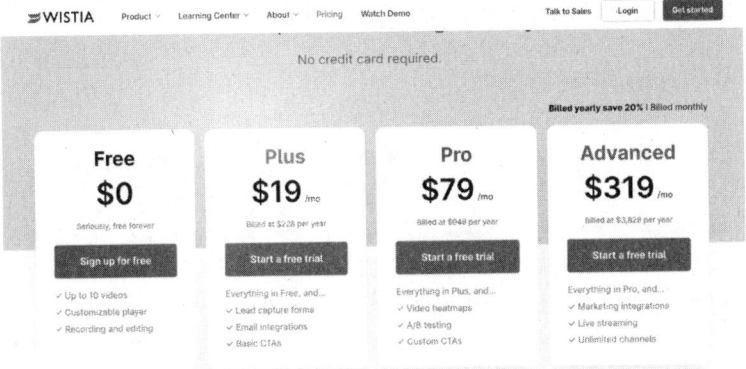

Usage-based Pricing

SaaS companies sometimes charge based on what a customer uses in a given month. This is a usage-based pricing model.

The advantage of this model is that customers only pay for what they use and don't think that they are underutilizing their subscription.

However, with usage-based pricing, customers may need help accurately predicting how much they will use in a given month, making it harder to estimate their costs for the SaaS product or service. In addition, usage doesn't always equate to the value delivered to the customer, which is why there is a misalignment between cost and value.

AWS offers a usage-based pricing model. Customers pay for the amount of storage capacity they use in a given month. There are two different workload types, and the cost per GB for each is different. This pricing model benefits customers because they only pay for the capacity they use for storage. However, unless they know exactly how much storage they will need in the future, they cannot predict their future costs.

How do you pay for AWS?

Pay-as-you-go

Pay-as-you-go allows you to easily adapt to changing business needs without overcommitting budgets and improving your responsiveness to changes. With a pay-as-you-go model, you can adapt your business depending on need and not on forecasts, reducing the risk of overprovisioning or missing capacity.

Read more »

Save when you commit

For AWS Compute and AWS Machine Learning, Savings Plans offer savings over On-Demand in exchange for a commitment to use a specific amount (measured in $/hour) of an AWS service or a category of services, for a one- or three-year period.

Read more »

Pay less by using more

With AWS, you can get volume based discounts and realize important savings as your usage increases. For services such as S3, pricing is tiered, meaning the more you use, the less you pay per GB. AWS also gives you options to acquire services that help you address your business needs.

Read more »

Type of Workload	EFS TCO ($/GB-mo)	EFS TCO ($/GB-mo)	EFS Savings (%) *	Description
General Purpose	$0.0315	$0.0797	60%	An EFS workload leveraging SSD, Infrequent Access, and Archive storage classes with Elastic Throughput
Serverless	$0.2172	$1.3822	84%	Workload with short-lived, ephemeral data leveraging SSD storage and Elastic Throughput.

Value-based Pricing

The third type of pricing model is value-based pricing. In this model, customers only pay for the value they receive from using the SaaS product. This could be in revenue gained, user service or some other value metric.

The most significant advantage of this model is that the price paid is fully aligned with the value that the customer gets from the product or service. If a customer receives less value in a given month, they will spend less, and conversely, the more value they get, the more they will pay.

There are, however, two significant challenges affecting this model. First, it can be challenging to measure value in a quantitative way for all products, so most SaaS companies use the closest proxy for actual value delivered. For instance, it is hard to know how much value a customer gets from workplace communication using Slack vs email. Instead, they use a close proxy of the 'active user' on the platform.

Second, the customer's willingness to pay for the same value metric might differ greatly, so choosing the right price point per unit of value can take time and effort. This is why value-based pricing is less standard than other monetization strategies.

HubSpot, for instance, charges based on marketing contacts—or the actual contacts to whom a customer sends an email or ad through HubSpot. This is the closest proxy to value delivered for a HubSpot customer, but it still isn't a perfect proxy.

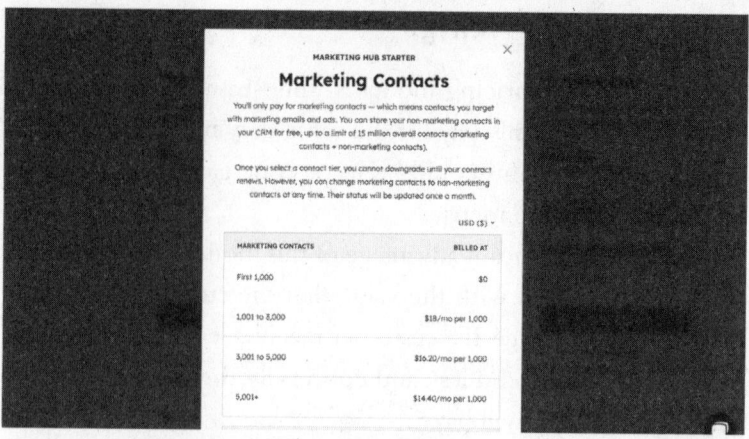

Another example is Amplitude, which is a data analytics platform. They charge based on 'Monthly Tracked Users,' or the number of users being tracked through the data platform and dashboards by Amplitude's customers. This works as a proxy for the value they are getting from Amplitude because it enables them to take the right actions on their products for activation, retention, loyalty and lifetime value.

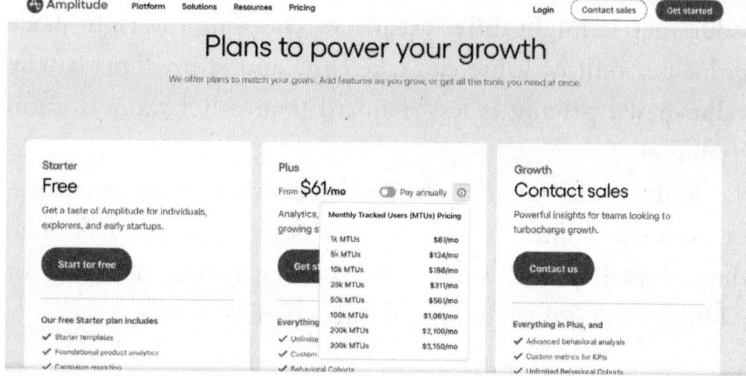

Hybrid Pricing Models

Many SaaS companies use a hybrid of feature-differentiated and either usage- or value-based pricing. They have a few different pricing tiers based on varying feature sets, and then the price scales with a usage or value metric.

For example, Intercom's pricing combines usage-based and feature-differentiated pricing. There are three different tiers based on the features available, and the price is set per seat—a product usage metric.

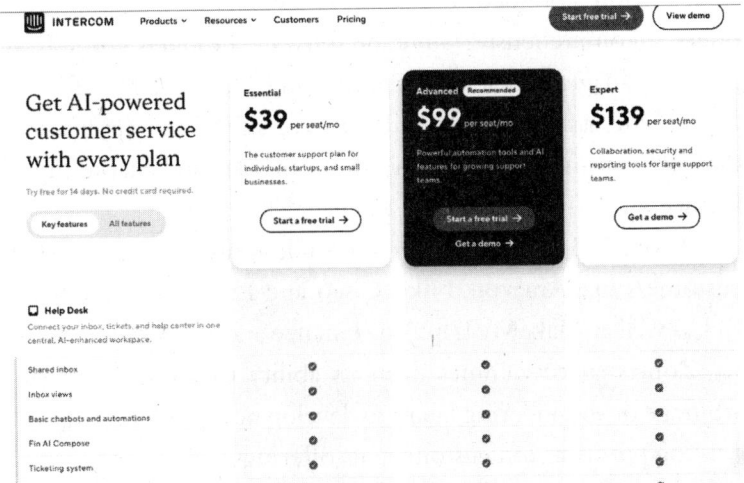

Finally, it is worth noting that pricing isn't a one-off decision that SaaS companies can set and forget. The pricing model needs to evolve along with the changing customer segments, customer needs and product offerings, the ability of the company to track usage or value delivered, and the preferences and sophistication of target customers and the sector as a whole.

The Rise of SaaS in India

Over the last decade, India has emerged as a significant player in the SaaS ecosystem, serving a market of ~$13 billion ARR as of 2022, projected to grow to a $25 billion ARR industry by 2030.[2]

These Indian SaaS companies are well regarded in their respective industries and product categories, competing globally and serving Fortune 500 customers like Toyota, FedEx and Bridgestone.

The best example of an Indian SaaS success story is Zoho Corporation. Founded in 1996 in Chennai, India, the company offers a comprehensive suite of software products for CRM, project management and email marketing. Their flagship offering, Zoho One, is a unified cloud software suite with applications that support many business needs, from sales and marketing to finance and HR operations.

As of 2023, Zoho has over 100 million users across 7,00,000 customers like Amazon, Nike, Cisco and FedEx in the US and EU, as well as MakeMyTrip, Axis Finance and BigBasket in India.

Zoho's success comes from its ability to leverage its geo-arbitrage on engineering talent to develop new products, improve existing products and customize its offerings to industry-specific use cases, all at a highly competitive price point. In addition, their go-to-market strategy of product-led growth helps them leverage their strength in product development to acquire new customers, instead of relying solely on expensive sales teams to grow their customer base.

---

[2] 'SaaS Capital', *SaaS Capital*, 13 November 2024, https://www.saas-capital.com/

Tailwinds to the Indian SaaS Ecosystem

Several tailwinds propelled the growth of the Indian SaaS ecosystem.

First, the advent of cloud computing and internet access enabled Indian companies to serve any customer across the globe reliably and at high speeds.

Second, India offers a substantial cost arbitrage in product development. This cost arbitrage is partly fuelled by access to a vast pool of technical talent with experience in global and Indian software companies and partly by the cultural tendency towards frugality and efficiency. This has enabled Indian SaaS companies to build products more quickly and cost-effectively than their global counterparts.

Third, the Indian government introduced policies like Digital India to promote the start-up ecosystem and the growth of start-ups, creating an environment conducive to the growth of new SaaS start-ups.

Fourth, investor and industry confidence in Indian SaaS companies has grown significantly, with Indian SaaS companies raising ~$6 billion in investments in 2022, a 3.5x growth from 2020 and an 8x growth from 2018. Venture capitalists like Accel Partners and Nexus have been especially bullish on Indian SaaS, investing a significant share of their funds in Indian SaaS and cloud providers.

Factors Driving Success of Indian SaaS Companies

The success of an Indian SaaS company is a tale of two strategies.

Some Indian SaaS companies like Zoho, Freshdesk and Chargebee have taken a global-first approach. They started targeting customers in the US, UK and Europe and built products to compete with global SaaS players. These companies were able to differentiate on cost with access to highly talented but lower-cost resources across engineering, product and go-to-market and sales while increasing velocity with larger teams and the hustle mindset.

Yet other Indian SaaS companies like Perfios and Razorpay started by serving Indian customers. These companies offered more personalized products to the Indian context than their global competitors and were more effective and user-friendly than traditional Indian IT service providers. This enabled them to build their product with Indian customers and expand globally to Southeast Asia, the Middle East and other geographies over time.

Chargebee is an Indian subscription billing platform serving global and Indian companies. They offer integrations with Indian payment gateways and support for Indian tax regulations, enabling them to compete effectively with global subscription platforms like Zuora and Recurly.

Future of SaaS

SaaS as a business model and product category has reached a point of maturity and will continue to grow. However, the future of SaaS will look very different from what the industry has looked like over the last decade.

Democratization of Product Development

Over the last four to five years, no-code and low-code solutions have made it easier than ever to build software products. Tools like bubble.io offer powerful no-code platforms that allow non-technical people to create fully functional web applications without coding. Another example is Airtable, a no-code database solution that non-technical users can utilize to build simple applications for tasks like project management, CRM and inventory tracking.

In addition, the advancement of generative AI has further accelerated this trend. AI can translate natural language instructions into coding language to help test and debug code. This enables non-technical users to describe the functionality they need and iteratively build applications without learning how to code, thus obviating the need for expert technical teams to accelerate the development, testing and launch of applications.

This has a few interesting implications. First, the barrier to entry to build and launch a product is a lot lower than it was even in 2020. This will lead to a proliferation of new entrants in the SaaS market. Second, larger incumbents who were previously slow to innovate are moving faster and launching new products and features at an incredible velocity. This is most obvious in the AI solution space—with incumbents like Adobe launching AI features soon after new disruptors enter the market. Third, users now expect more customizable and adaptable solutions that they can tailor to serve their specific needs and use cases.

As a result, the competition in the SaaS industry will get even more substantial, while the rising customer expectations will make it harder to acquire and retain customers. Incumbents who can quickly adopt and use AI in their workflows and evolve their product strategy to meet changing customer needs are most likely to succeed.

Implications for India

For India, this has another implication. Cost arbitrage on product development will disappear or get lower.

Cost arbitrage for Indian companies will get lower due to advancements in no-code and low-code platforms, generative

AI and automation, which reduce the need for extensive technical expertise and make software development accessible and affordable globally. These technologies lower the barriers to entry for software creation, allowing companies in higher cost regions to develop products more efficiently in-house, thus diminishing the cost advantage traditionally enjoyed by Indian firms. Indian SaaS companies need to first and foremost adopt AI and proactively use it to sharpen their competitive advantage in product development further. In addition, they need to find other axes of differentiation beyond cost competitiveness to differentiate themselves in the global market.

Verticalization of SaaS

Vertical SaaS solutions have been growing in popularity, offering greater value to customers and enabling SaaS providers to differentiate themselves from horizontal incumbents.

This trend will only grow in importance as customers become savvier and demand solutions that serve their unique needs. Moreover, as SaaS becomes more accepted by traditional industries like construction, financial services and healthcare, with industry-specific workflows and needs, the opportunity for vertical solutions will further skyrocket.

These vertical SaaS companies will be able to penetrate their target industries more deeply, with larger market shares. They will also see more excellent retention and customer loyalty as they can deliver more value with customized products, expand into adjacent use cases for their target industry and evolve their product with customers' changing needs.

Horizontal SaaS companies who want to capitalize on this trend can build on their product expertise and expand into industry-specific solutions. Salesforce, for instance, has always been a horizontal CRM platform. Recently, they have verticalized their offerings with Salesforce Health Cloud for the healthcare industry and Salesforce Financial Services Cloud for the finance industry.

The SaaS sector offers immense growth potential for budding entrepreneurs, thanks to lower barriers to entry facilitated by no-code and low-code platforms and generative AI. These advancements allow non-technical founders to rapidly develop and launch software products. Additionally, the global expansion of cloud-based solutions creates opportunities across various industries. Entrepreneurs can capitalize on this by developing specialized vertical SaaS solutions tailored to niche markets like healthcare and finance, fostering deeper market penetration and customer loyalty. Emerging technologies like AI, ML and blockchain further enhance SaaS capabilities, enabling innovative and efficient solutions. By leveraging these trends, entrepreneurs can create cutting-edge products and succeed in the evolving SaaS landscape.

Key Takeaways

SaaS has revolutionized how software is delivered and consumed and fundamentally altered the dynamics of business operations across industries.

The key takeaways from our discussion underscore the transformative impact of SaaS on businesses and industries at large:

1. Democratization of Technology: SaaS has levelled the playing field, enabling start-ups and small businesses to access the same powerful tools that are available to large enterprises, fostering innovation and competition across the board.

2. Cost Efficiency and Flexibility: By shifting from capital expenditures to operational expenditures, SaaS offers businesses the flexibility to scale services up or down based on demand, significantly reducing overall costs and increasing efficiency.
3. Global Reach and Accessibility: The cloud-based nature of SaaS solutions means that businesses can now operate and serve customers globally without needing a physical presence or substantial infrastructure investments in new markets.
4. Continuous Innovation and Improvement: SaaS providers continuously update and improve their offerings, ensuring that businesses can always access the latest features and security enhancements without needing manual upgrades.
5. Customer-centric Model: The SaaS model emphasizes customer satisfaction and value over upfront sales, encouraging providers to prioritize user experience, reliability and support.

The SaaS model is poised for continued growth and evolution as we look to the future. Emerging technologies such as artificial intelligence, machine learning and blockchain are further set to enhance the capabilities and efficiencies of SaaS offerings. Moreover, the ongoing shift towards more specialized, industry-specific SaaS solutions indicates a deepening penetration into all sectors of the economy, promising even more personalized and efficient service delivery.

6

Fintech

Many of us have grown up with the experience of standing in queues at ration shops and bringing back heavy bags of our monthly supplies of subsidized rice, sugar, wheat, etc. With the advent of direct benefit transfer, this has reduced significantly. The proliferation of bank accounts, digital transfer of funds and digital payments has made access to financial services easier and frictionless. Getting a personal loan or a mortgage used to take many trips to the bank branch and files of documents to be submitted and followed up on. Today you can get personal loans in minutes and a mortgage in hours without having to make repeated trips to the bank. This radical transformation in access to financial services has taken place due to the emergence of a new category of financial services companies.

The financial services industry has been an early adopter of technology and has relied on technology to support its complex and distributed operating models.

However, we have seen the emergence of a new breed of financial services companies which are built on the strength of new digital technologies. These companies are disrupting the way financial services are offered and consumed by both B2C and B2B. They have also created new service types and have reached new audiences. This category of companies is referred to as fintechs.

India has been one of the leaders in the growth of fintechs due to several enabling factors that we will talk about in the coming sections.

The slide below, with information sourced from the BCG Matrix partners' report on fintechs, showcases India's position in the fintech sector.

India amongst top three globally on Fintech strength, funding and deal volume

	USA	UK	India	Canada	China	Australia
# Fintechs as on Jul'23	34034	12775	10244	3965	3717	3639
CAGR (# Fintechs) (2020–2023)	11%	10%	14%	10%	5%	6%
Funding ($) (Jul'18–Jul'23)	225 Bn	63 Bn	25 Bn	10.5 Bn	20 Bn	8.6 Bn
# Deals (Jul'18–Jul'23)	6,562	2,184	2,236	572	589	346
#Unicorns as on Jul'23	170	37	25	7	38	3

Source: Tracxn data as on Jul'23, Cumulative data from Jul'18 to Jul'23

The growth of fintechs has taken place primarily across banking, payment, lending, insurance and wealth management. We have also seen them emerge in the area of providing SaaS platforms to enable financial services in the SME sector.

Enabling Factors for Growth of Fintech in India

The fintech innovation in India is an excellent example of a confluence of multiple forces. Indian entrepreneurs have been very proactive in using these opportunities to build companies across multiple segments of the industry.

The widespread availability of smartphones and access to the Internet have been important factors in the growth of digital industries in India. Fintech is one of the industries that has been built on this foundation. By 2020, India had over 700 million internet users, with some of the world's cheapest data plans. This has encouraged Indian users across the country, including remote villages and tribal locations, to use the smartphone to access education, entertainment, health and financial services.

Paytm, an Indian digital payments and financial services company, exemplifies this trend. Founded in 2010, it capitalized on the growing number of smartphone users, offering a user-friendly platform for digital payments, which later expanded into wealth management and distribution of financial services, including credit and insurance.

Another catalyst for fintech growth in India was the government's push towards digitalization and financial inclusion. The launch of UPI in 2016 by the National Payments Corporation of India revolutionized digital payments, allowing instant, real-time transactions across different bank accounts. This was a game changer, enabling start-ups like PhonePe and Google Pay to offer seamless peer-to-peer transfer services.

Globally, similar developments were unfolding. In China, companies like Alipay and WeChat Pay transformed the payments landscape, leveraging the country's high smartphone penetration.

In the US, companies like Square and Stripe emerged, simplifying payments processing for businesses and consumers.

The Indian fintech landscape also witnessed a surge in innovation due to the 'India Stack'—a set of Application Programming Interfaces (API) that allow governments, businesses, start-ups and developers to utilize a unique digital infrastructure to solve the problems that India encountered on its way to presenceless, paperless and cashless service delivery. Aadhaar, a twelve-digit unique identity number issued to Indian residents based on their biometric and demographic data, played a pivotal role. It enabled fintech companies like Paytm and others to offer Know Your Customer (KYC) solutions swiftly and efficiently, dramatically reducing the cost and time of customer onboarding.

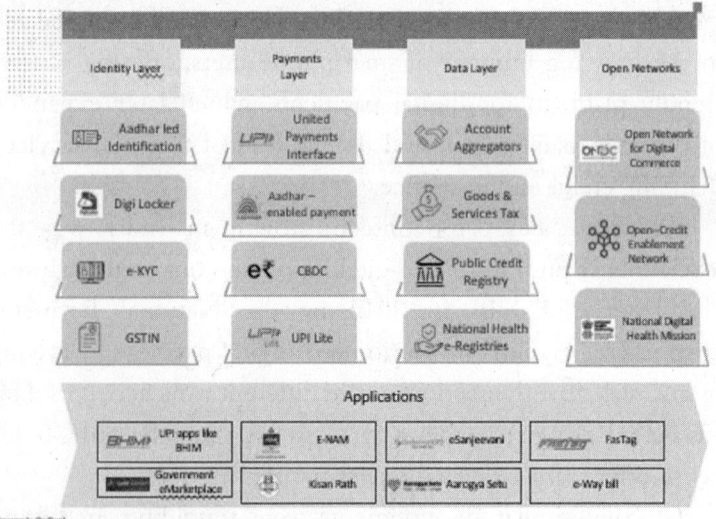

India's unique digital public infrastructure is the poster child for global disruption and has enabled rapid Fintech growth

Regulatory changes have also been made over the last decade, such as Goods and Services Tax, e-invoicing, regulatory sandboxes for live, closed testing of innovations, etc. have been helpful too. The regulator has been continuously providing inputs on the framework for digital transactions, payments and insurance tech.

With these enabling factors, investors were not far behind. The Venture Capital (VC)/Private Equity (PE) industry played a critical role in driving the innovation and growth of the fintech industry. Companies like BharatPe, Pine Labs and Razorpay have raised very large sums of money to build and grow their companies. Similarly, global fintech start-ups like Robinhood Markets in the US and Klarna in Sweden have raised substantial funds, allowing them to disrupt traditional financial models and expand their user base.

Dimensions of Fintech Innovation

One of the biggest signs of change in the financial services industry is visible in the payments space. Digital wallets and virtual payments are now the norm across the country, including the smallest of shops and in the remotest of places. With Paytm, PhonePe and Google Pay getting a big boost during COVID-19, this transformation is here to stay. Companies like Razorpay and Pine Labs have enabled companies and merchants to carry out their financial transactions digitally.

We see similar trends in the US with Venmo and Paypal making digital payments frictionless. In Kenya, m-Pesa, a mobile-based payment transfer system, has helped provide better access to financial services to a large section of the population, not covered by the traditional banking system.

The second area of change that we see is related to access to credit. By analysing data obtained from multiple sources, fintechs have been able to better understand the creditworthiness of customers and offer different types of credit, including Buy

Now, Pay Later, Pay Day Credit, Peer-to-Peer Lending, etc. Cred, a credit card payment platform, has used its data analytics capabilities to offer rewards and benefits to its customers, increasing engagement substantially.

Neobanks, which are completely digital in nature, provide the entire range of banking services without any physical branches. They tend to collaborate with traditional banks in order to be able to surmount the regulatory barriers by using the banking licence of the latter.

Insurance is another area that has seen transformation, with a number of discovery and aggregator platforms like Policy Bazaar, and also digital-first insurance companies such as Digit.

Another area that is developing is 'banking as a service' and other infrastructure solutions to enable the digitalization of traditional financial services companies such as Non-Banking Financial Companies (NBFCs). M2P Fintech and Zeta are examples of such companies in India. Stripe, a US-based company, has been very active in helping banks and other financial institutions offer digital-only credit and debit cards through its infrastructure solutions. This is apart from their core business of enabling payment solutions of various kinds to businesses that wish to carry out digital payments for their transactions.

Areas related to wealth management, investment and share trading have undergone changes with the arrival of fintechs. Zerodha is an excellent example of this segment. They have been able to make trading in the stock market accessible to many customers. Robinhood in the US is another such example.

Regulatory changes have been taking place alongside the development of fintechs, to ensure that financial services companies are managing their risks appropriately. Traditional banking and other financial services companies come under a great deal of regulation from Securities and Exchange Board of India (SEBI), Reserve Bank of India (RBI) and Insurance Regulatory and

Development Authority of India (IRDAI). The fintechs have tried to build their businesses around these regulations. However, over the last few years, the regulators have been paying a lot of attention to the fintech start-ups and building stronger regulatory frameworks. In September 2022, RBI introduced the Digital Lending guidelines and released the Frequently Asked Questions (FAQs) in February 2023. These are applicable to the 'digital lending apps' of regulated entities such as banks and NBFCs as well as the 'lending service provider', which are front-end organizations/start-ups, who source and service customers looking to borrow funds.

Payments Revolution

One of the most visible changes in the financial services industry is seen in the area of payments. There has been a remarkable shift from cash and credit card payments to digital payments of many forms. These range from digital wallets to peer-to-peer payments, Quick Response (QR) based payments, etc.

The demonetization of Rs500 and Rs1000 currency notes in 2016, combined with the widespread adoption of smartphones, has provided the foundation for the rapid adoption of digital financial transactions. Paytm (an acronym for Pay through mobile) had started even before demonetization, as a wallet-based online mobile and Direct-to-Home (DTH) recharge service. Over time, it became one of the most popular digital wallets, enabling customers to pay for various online purchases. Using the jingle 'Paytm karo' (use Paytm), the company popularized the concept of digital payments using their wallet.

In April 2016, a pilot launch of the UPI system was carried out with twenty-one member banks. UPI is an interface that maps our mobile numbers to our bank accounts, and allows for peer and person-to-merchant payments using just a mobile app. Using this capability created by the NCPI and regulated by RBI, we are able to make payments through Google Pay, PhonePe and Bharat Interface for Money (BHIM). Most online commerce sites integrate UPI into their key payment methods. The advantage of UPI is its simplicity; we can make payments without having to share bank details with the receiver each time. However, this means that our accounts are immediately debited, and, unlike credit cards, we don't have the opportunity to pay later. UPI is seen as a very innovative payment system globally, and now India is working with a few countries, including Sri Lanka, Singapore, Mauritius, etc. to help them adopt it.

While payment apps do not charge for the actual UPI transactions, they have built a revenue model around this. PhonePe charges the merchants for the Point of Sale (POS) payment capability through which they can receive payments through UPI, credit and debit cards. PhonePe has several services integrated into its app, ranging from insurance to wealth management to cross-border fund transfers. Recently they also created a hyperlocal e-commerce shopping site called Pincode, using Open Network for Digital Commerce (ONDC).

Payment apps collect a huge amount of data related to the spending patterns of their customers; this gives them another opportunity to earn revenue, through advertising and the products and services of their partners. PhonePe offers a service called 'switch' through which customers can access a number of partner apps seamlessly, through a single login.

UPI-based payment systems have been instrumental in increasing the access to digital payments in India, as a wide range of customers, who had not used credit/debit cards earlier, have now moved away from cash payments.

Digital payments have transformed the way merchants operate. The smallest of merchants in remote locations have now enabled QR codes through which they are able to receive cashless payments. BharatPe is one of the key fintechs that has played an important role in this. This has significantly reduced the friction at the customer end. Especially during COVID-19, this capability was instrumental in continuing commerce and has remained a preferred option since then. Digital payments at the merchant end help reduce cash management complexity and costs, making the accounting of financial transactions much easier. This is particularly helpful for SMBs.

However, the growth of digital payments also presents challenges, particularly in terms of security and privacy. As transactions move online, concerns over data breaches, fraud and cyberattacks have increased. Consequently, payment service providers are continuously enhancing their security measures, employing technologies like blockchain and AI to safeguard transactions and user data.

Phishing/vishing are some of the techniques used to obtain the credentials of a customer fraudulently and using those credentials to withdraw funds from their accounts. Fake QR codes are used to divert funds into wrong accounts. Mule accounts are created by getting the credentials of customers and using their accounts to transfer funds fraudulently and move them to other locations/accounts.

Lending Solutions

As the Indian economy continues its impressive growth, it gives rise to a substantial demand in credit. Consumers are more upwardly mobile and are looking for various credit products to fund their lifestyles and growing needs. Equally, the large numbers of the fast-growing category of SMEs and micro enterprises are looking to fund their expansion through credit.

India's credit penetration in the MSME segment is 14 per cent, compared to 50 per cent in the US and 37 per cent in

China. Retail loans in India are at 11 per cent, compared to 75 per cent in the US and 55 per cent in China (EY report on Digital Lending, September 2023).

In this huge opportunity, digital lending solutions have jumped in to ride this wave, with a 12x growth in digital lending between 2017 and 2020, Digital lending is expected to grow at a CAGR of 22 per cent in the next three to four years, compared to 12 per cent growth in traditional lending.

Digital lending is offered by some of the more tech-savvy traditional banks. However, there are a number of new lending tech companies, NBFCs and neobanks. This new form of lending tends to use enhanced credit scoring, using alternative data sources and AI/ML algorithms, and is hence able to reach out to newer customer segments, both for retail and commercial lending. The journey of acquiring customers and enabling them to complete their credit journey and fulfil their payments tends to be completely digital, leading to significantly improved turnaround times and reduced friction, resulting in improved customer experience.

The lending tech industry has innovated in multiple dimensions. These include the data providers who support the acquisition and qualification/underwriting of the risk of the potential credit seekers. In the consumer lending space, companies like Paisabazaar offer a marketplace where customers can shop for loans. Amazon and Flipkart have built in embedded credit through Buy Now, Pay Later (BNPL) solutions in their workflow. There are companies like Rupeek that provide gold loans, personal loans, LazyPay and Simpl provide BNPL solutions, while LiquiLoans provides P2P lending services.

In the MSME space, there are companies like LendingKart that provide loans to SMEs, bill discounting companies such as KredX, revenue-based lending (a percentage of gross revenue is taken by the loan provider) like Velocity, merchant cash advance providers like Flexiloans, etc.

Through these innovative products and alternative methods of credit evaluation, fintechs have a much higher share of the 'New to Credit' customer base in India. This, of course, also means that fintechs are catering to customers with lower credit scores, which is riskier by nature.

Government initiatives, including Aadhar, DigiLocker and UPI, have certainly helped in the growth of the lendingtech industry. Additionally, the Account Aggregator (AA) platforms and the TReDS platform (Trade receivables discount system) have helped the MSME segments to get easier credit access.

The table below shows how the lending journey has been transformed.

Digital lending value chain	What has changed?	Technologies and innovations that are endorsing accelerated transformation of lending into value based process
Prospecting Borrower scans through specialized lenders and products and selects the best option	**More variety:** Digital lenders offer competitive interest rates and specialized product suit for borrowers to compare from	► Partnerships ► Integration of APIs with RPA ► Biometric identity verification ► Big data analytics
Onboarding Borrower interacts with multilingual chatbots and provides basic details to track identity online	**Convenient and quick application process:** Borrowers apply for loans online. The process is simple, and the application is completed in minutes	► Multilingual chatbot ► AA framework ► Video KYC, facematch ► Liveness detection, OCR
Underwriting Lenders make use of alternative data sources to assess credibility	**Quick assessment of credit worthiness:** Digital lenders use advanced algorithms to process applications - loan approval takes few minutes, funds disbursed in few hours	► Alternative data sources ► Affluence score ► Satellite image analysis ► Social media activity
Disbursement Borrower is onboarded online	**Transparent lending process:** Borrowers use digital platforms to track loan application status in real-time	► User friendly mobile apps ► Blockchain ► 100% cloud-based infrastructure ► Internet of things
Repayment Borrower uses the network and power of digital payments	**Automated and hassle-free payments:** Digital lenders provide flexible repayment options - online, pre-approved payment facilities, automatic debits	► The power of digital payments ► Initiatives such as eNACH

Source: 'Unleashing potential: The Next Phase of Digital Lending in India', *EY*, September 2023.

BNPL has emerged as a key credit journey driven by the growth of e-commerce. Most e-commerce sites now provide BNPL offerings embedded in the buying process. A few like Amazon have built their own BNPL offerings, while many have collaborated with BNPL providers such as LazyPay and Simpl. These BNPL solutions provide small credits for short durations. Mobile wallets also provide revolving credit as per the limits they have set for the customer.

Usage of AI and advanced data analytics can help in improving the journey of digital lending from prospecting and underwriting to better risk management by proactively identifying potential repayment issues.

Insurtech

Insurtech stands for technology-led insurance industry providers. Insurance, one of the most traditional and regulated industries, is undergoing transformation with digital technology.

There are four key areas of digital transformation that the large insurance majors are going through:

1. Digital products and services, directly and through ecosystem partnerships: These include complete digital journeys with dynamic pricing based on events and situations. Making the entire renewal process frictionless and automating it has helped to improve the product experience.
2. Data analysis: Using advanced analytics to improve the quality of underwriting and reduce risk, as well as using the data to create more customized products for micro markets.
3. Omnichannel customer experience: This means targeting and acquiring customers through multiple channels and also to service them through their channel of preference.

4. Automated operations: This refers to the use of technology to improve the quality of operations, to improve customer response times and also to reduce costs.

Insurtechs are taking this transformation to the next level by bringing about disruption in distribution, risk coverage and customer experience. Apart from digital technology, IoT devices and AI are playing an important role in this disruption.

Distribution is one of the early areas of transformation that the insurtech companies have brought to the market. Policybazaar, founded in 2008, is one of the earliest competitors in this field. They are an insurance aggregator, helping customers evaluate multiple insurance products across various areas of risk, ranging from general insurance to motor vehicle insurance to health insurance. Their model has been predominantly call-centre-led and due to this, they have an all-India reach. They listed the company a couple of years ago. Turtlemint is another well-funded company, which has taken a slightly different approach. They have used technology to train and enable insurance advisors to offer the best solutions to their customers. While they do have a direct-to-consumer interface, they help connect customers to advisors to get the expertise they need to decide on the most suitable product for them. Recently, InsuranceDekho, started by the founders of CarDekho, has raised substantial funds for a model that is highly field-force-led. They are focusing on a large population of uninsured customers in the Tier II and Tier III markets. In these markets, the expectation is to have a face-to-face conversation with an insurance advisor, rather than with a call centre advisor.

Digital underwriting is another area that has seen some strong players like Acko and Digit emerge. Acko, founded in 2016, offers a complete digital journey for customers in the general insurance industry, and lately also in health insurance. While they acquire customers directly, they also work extensively with ecosystem partners by embedding themselves in the product journey of their partners. This allows them to offer their products at the time of the purchase of products, or when travel or other events arise. Being contextual helps them to be more effective in acquiring customers at a lower cost of acquisition. Using data analytics, these companies are able to offer customized and cost-effective products to their beneficiaries. They have been able to reduce the turnaround time for the issuance of new policies and for paying out claims. Using blockchain technology has helped them across the journey with smart contracting, cost savings and fraud mitigation.

Specialised insurance SaaS providers such as Riskcovry and Ensuredit have emerged to support the digital transformation of the insurance industry. Riskcovry supports insurance brokers, other Banking, Financial Services and Insurance (BFSI) companies, and any enterprise/e-commerce clients that wish to offer insurance solutions to their customers. Ensuredit offers Platform as a Service to enable POS agents, corporate agents, insurers and distributors to build their customer acquisition journeys. They provide API connectivity to a number of general and health insurers to offer an end-to-end digital journey for onboarding new customers.

Digital corporate insurance brokers such as Nova Benefits and Plum work with corporates to help them manage the insurance requirements of their employees. They help with setting up the most suitable insurance plan for the employees as a group, followed by onboarding and claims management, all done seamlessly through the digital platform. They provide dashboards for employees as well as for the corporate. In addition, they offer a number of health and wellness services to the employees, e.g., annual health checks, tele-consultation, wellness programmes, trackers for chronic diseases, etc. They have features that help corporate clients to manage administrative tasks related to employee health and insurance benefits. They create engaging front ends/apps to enable the employees to increase their engagement with health and wellness and to manage their insurance in a simple and user-friendly format.

Data analytics play a vital role in the operations of insurtech companies. This helps them to improve their operations, enhance their customer experience and make better business decisions.

By analysing historical data on past frauds, during the onboarding process and later, statistical models can help predict and avoid frauds. Data helps target the marketing and helps in customizing products to microsegments, while managing the risk profile of the portfolio. With the help of data from IoT devices, e.g., sensors in wearables, it is possible to track and nudge insurance customers to follow a more health consonant lifestyle which could potentially improve the claims ratios. AI-based solutions companies, such as Artivatic, help with auto adjudication of health insurance claims.

Neobanks

Neobanks are digital-only banks, which emerged in the period following the 2008 financial crisis. They are also referred to as 'challenger banks' as they are competing with the traditional banks by targeting younger and more digital savvy customers.

They are mobile-first, establishing relationships with customers primarily through digital channels across multiple products. They normally don't have any branches. Pure play neobanks tend to focus more on customer experience, primarily on acquiring and servicing customers. They ride on the banking license of the traditional bank and depend on traditional banks for the underwriting of loans and for providing the capital for the loans. Some of the neobanks are also NBFCs and have their own line of funds available for credit relationships.

Neobanks offer the traditional products of savings and credit, but may also offer more innovative products and services such as peer-to-peer lending, crypto, automatic financial advisory, etc. They target both individuals and SMEs by offering products and services that make day-to-day operations easier. For instance, expense tracking of individuals as well as employees in an SME, by connecting to the debit cards that have been issued by the bank, can help reduce the administrative burden.

Typical Products and Services for Individual Customers Include:

Offerings for SMEs cover:

Due to their digital-only nature, their ability to collect data about their customers is superior; data analytics can be very helpful for further building on their customer relationships. To acquire new customers and to qualify them, data from multiple sources is used. They are able to attract a new generation of young tech-savvy people into the banking industry and help them build their credit journeys.

Jupiter, Niyo and Open are some Indian neobanks. However, these neobanks are still small with revenues ranging from Rs50 to Rs200 crore per annum. Some of the top global neobanks include Nubank from Brazil, Revolut from the UK and KakaoBank from South Korea.

The neobanks do not have any legacy banking systems to contend with and have the flexibility to build very nimble and customer-friendly front ends.

With the popularity of neobanks, traditional banks have started building digital banks too. These are complete end-to-end digital accounts offered as a separate brand in many cases. These include 811 from Kotak, Yono from SBI and Axis Open from Axis Bank. These neobanks use a new technology platform for the front end while building connections with the existing banking systems for their bank end processing. Digital banks emerging from traditional bank set-ups have the benefit of being funded and supported by the parent, while neobanks have to raise funding from PEs to grow and survive.

Several neobanks have started and shut down due to their inability to become sustainable.

The last few years have been challenging for neobanks that have focused solely on growth and not on profitability. In the last twelve months, as many new launches have been seen as close downs, leading to the number of nearly 400 neobanks staying constant. There have been a significant number of mergers and strategic acquisitions, and complete shutdowns during the last few years.

Payment Banks

These are a regulated and licensed category of banks, meant only to provide a facility for receiving and making payments. This is a new type of financial institution that was introduced in India in 2014. They provide basic banking services to people who are currently unbanked or underbanked. Payment banks cannot offer loans or credit cards. They can only offer savings accounts, current accounts and mobile banking services.

These banks operate with minimum credit risk as they are only permitted to take deposits and facilitate payment. The maximum deposit that a bank can hold is Rs2 lakh per depositor.

There is a restriction on the way the deposits can be deployed by the banks; they have to hold 75 per cent as government securities and the balance as commercial bank time deposits.

These banks can offer mobile banking services, domestic remittance services, i.e., sending and receiving payments. They offer debit cards and ATM cards for cash withdrawals. Through partnerships, they may offer insurance and investment products such as mutual funds.

They tend to operate digital first and have a high volume and low value of transactions.

While payment banks are helpful in bringing in the unbanked population into banking services, their capabilities are quite limited.

Airtel Payments Bank was one of the earliest payment banks in India. Some of the well-known payment banks in India include India Post, Fino Payments Bank, Jio Payments Bank and NSDL Payments Bank.

Over the years, payment banks have diversified their fee earning opportunities. While they earn through the difference in the interest rate between the deposits they hold and the investments they make, there are other mechanisms that have evolved. There could be charges for the payments of various bills, including utilities, DTH, telecom, etc. Small fees may be levied for services on the accounts. Offering a number of products and services through partnerships is a key approach used by many. Airtel Payments Bank even sells a smartwatch on their site; apart from functioning as a watch and fitness band, the smartwatch can also be used to make and receive payments. You can also use it to buy and recharge FASTags for your vehicles.

They have also come up with services for merchants to be able to facilitate easy receipt of payments through QR codes. They offer salary and reimbursement solutions for SMEs and small corporates.

Data monetization is a possible avenue of revenue generation. Payment banks tend to cater to a new generation of customers who hitherto may not have been accessing regular banking services. Through the transactions that go through their system, the payment banks have access to fairly detailed income and spending pattern information of their customers, which would be potentially very useful for other players in the BFSI sector. They can provide aggregate data to players, across the BFSI and other sectors, who wish to understand customer behaviours for their product lines. With the consent of customers, the data of individual customers can be offered for specific cross-selling of other products.

Payment banks need to work in a very efficient mode to get to profitability, due to fewer avenues for monetization. Both Airtel and Jio benefit from the large telecom base for customer acquisition and that potentially makes it easier for them to grow and get to profitability.

Broking and Wealth Management

Wealthtech represents the convergence of financial assets with cutting-edge technology to offer innovative investment solutions and tools for managing finances. This sector is rapidly evolving, driven by increasing digital adoption and a growing base of tech-savvy investors. The Indian wealthtech market, valued at $23 billion in FY21, is projected to exceed $63 billion by 2025, highlighting its significant growth potential. https://redseer. com/reports/indian-wealthtech-a-60bn-opportunity-by-fy25/

Despite India's large population, only a very small portion, about 2–3 per cent, invests in the stock markets. This is in contrast with developed economies like the US, where approximately 55 per cent of the population engages in stock investments. This under-penetration presents a substantial opportunity for growth in the Indian wealthtech sector.

The key categories in this space include:

1. Digital Advisors

    Digital advisors are digital platforms that provide automated, algorithm-driven financial planning services with minimal human intervention. These platforms analyse risk tolerance, investment goals and market trends to create and manage customized investment portfolios for users.

    Scripbox, Fisdom and Kristal.ai are some of the key players in this space. Scripbox offers plans based on the goals that the customer may be chasing, e.g., education of children, purchase of some property or asset. Based on the goal and income generation capability of the individual, appropriate investment options (typically in mutual funds) are suggested and facilitated. Kristal.ai is a Singapore-headquartered company that offers a complete bouquet of private wealth management solutions on their digital platform. Betterment from the US offers automated investment services, helping users create and manage diversified portfolios based on their financial goals.

2. Digital Brokers or Investment Platforms

    Digital brokerage platforms offer consumers access to stock markets and investment vehicles, providing comprehensive investment-related information and tools for trading.

    Zerodha, Groww, INDmoney and Upstox are examples of Indian digital investment platforms. They provide low-cost investment services across multiple categories, ranging from stock markets to US stocks, to mutual funds and fixed deposits. They attract customers through their smooth digital interfaces, and low pricing options. However, as this space is heating up with traditional players such as the top commercial banks offering similar services at similar prices, there is revenue and profit pressure on these players. We see many of them now starting to create their own mutual funds and other products.

Robinhood Markets, a US-based player in this space, offers commission-free trading of stocks, Exchange Traded Funds and cryptocurrencies, democratizing access to financial markets.

3. Fractional Investment

Fractional investing is a vehicle through which multiple people can pool money so that they can create a large enough corpus to invest in high-value assets. These projects include real estate or lease-based debt models, art, inventory, etc.

Grip Invest and Smallcase are a few examples of companies that offer this product. The advantages of this model are small ticket sizes across multiple opportunities and easier liquidity. However, they tend to offer higher risk and higher returns.

Regulation and Governance

The evolution of the fintech industry has, in the past, been a race between innovation and regulatory oversight. A lot of the initial growth of the industry has been working around regulations. The banking and financial industry traditionally has been a highly regulated industry, with RBI, IRDAI and, of course, SEBI providing guard rails and the governance frameworks.

Many of the fintech players have worked outside the regulatory frameworks and have relied upon regulated entities to provide core financial services. In doing so, however, some challenges have emerged over the years; this is now the focus of the regulators.

KYC is an important requirement in the financial services industry. Regulated entities have to follow stringent checks to ensure that they are onboarding authentic customers. This is critical in order to reduce frauds, money laundering and non-performing assets.

The second critical area is constant monitoring and data analytics. Anti-money laundering aims to prevent terrorist financing and money laundering.

Ensuring that the data of individual customers is kept private and protected and all that sharing, if any, happens only after consent is obtained, is another important area of focus. The new Digital Personal Data Protection Act will have to be implemented very carefully by fintechs. Cybersecurity has become very important in the financial services sector, and fintechs need to build up capability to prevent and recover from any cyberattacks.

RBI has introduced guidelines to prevent predatory lending practices, with strong guidelines for disclosing all charges upfront for any loans being offered.

Payment banks need to obtain appropriate licenses from the RBI; they are closely supervised by RBI.

While these regulations are important to protect the business and the customers, they require substantial investment in process and technology on the part of the fintechs.

RBI also released a framework for a Self-Regulatory Organization (SRO) for fintechs. This will be an entity which will have fintechs as its members to formulate and ensure compliance with regulations that are appropriate to the entire basket of fintechs which are currently outside the ambit of RBI and IRDAI. Regulated entities, too, can join, if they so desire. However, others have to mandatorily be part of one of the SROs.

The central bank has put out six major mandates for the body: it needs to be truly representative of the sector; it should be a repository of data; encourage development; provide a platform for dispute resolution; encourage members to adhere to regulatory principles and be independent of influence. [1]

AI Impacting Fintech

AI and ML solutions are being utilized by fintechs in a variety of ways.

One of the first areas is improving customer experience. Customer support through a chatbot reduces the waiting times for basic queries and actions that need to be carried out for customers. Additionally, companies are adding AI co-pilots to the human customer service agents to improve the quality and comprehensiveness of the services provided.

Personalization of landing pages/mobile app, hyper personalization of products based on the insight provided through data analytics, modifying the flow in real time based on actions taken by customers—these are some examples of AI/ML usage.

---

[1] 'RBI Unveils Final Guidelines for Fintech SRO', *The Economic Times*, November 13, 2024, Tech & Internet section, https://economictimes.indiatimes.com/tech/technology/rbi-unveils-final-guidelines-for-fintech-sro-pci-wants-toapply/articleshow/110564648.cms

Creating innovative products such as robo-advisors and virtual relationship managers is another area that is gaining momentum. Using smart contracts and blockchain technology helps in reducing the friction in customer journey.

AI/ML has been deployed to help improve security and detect frauds early. By carrying out real-time analysis of transactions and mapping them to past patterns in data, it is possible to catch fraudulent transactions before they go through. Analysis of large volumes of data and the use of AI can help identify patterns and predict risks that might come up in the future.

Improvement in efficiency and accuracy of operations, using solutions such as robotic process automation (RPA) is gaining momentum. One example of this is automating the KYC process by extracting data from documents using Optical Character Recognition and comparing it with the information provided by the customer.

RPA can accelerate loan processing by automating the extraction and verification of information from loan applications, credit checks and employment verification. The time taken for credit scoring can be brought down from days to minutes by this technology.

The last decade has seen euphoria and exponential growth in the fintech industry. Very large amounts of investments have been made in this industry and India has emerged as one of the forerunners in this space. The digital public infrastructure laid by the government has been well exploited with the creation of innovative start-ups in this industry.

As we go forward, there are three dimensions in which the industry has to mature.

- Foster a DNA of compliance to regulatory norms. Design new products and offerings, keeping the regulatory requirements in mind.

- Move towards profitability by focusing on products and services that will provide the right margins. Growth will follow profitability.
- Collaborate extensively with existing regulated entities and create meaningful offerings which are based on a strong bedrock of risk management.

This industry has to move from the early stages of teenage exuberance to a mature and sustainable one. The next decade should see this transformation.

7

The Dawn of Direct-to-Consumer Brands

A young entrepreneur named Ananya has always been passionate about organic skincare. Frustrated by the lack of transparency and high prices in traditional retail stores, she decides to create her own line of products. Her vision is simple: to offer high-quality, natural skincare directly to consumers without the markups and gimmicks that often accompany the marketing of big, branded products.

With a modest budget, she begins by crafting her products in small batches in her home kitchen and selling them online. Ananya leverages social media to share her story, engaging with potential customers, and building a community around her brand. She partners with influencers who genuinely believe in her mission. Through word of mouth and genuine recommendations, her brand begins to gain traction.

Unlike traditional brands that rely on multiple layers of distribution, Ananya's direct-to-consumer (D2C) approach allowed her to communicate directly with her customers. She received immediate feedback, which she used to refine her products. Her customers appreciated the personal touch and the transparency of knowing exactly where their products came from and how they were made.

Within a year, Ananya's brand, 'Pure Radiance,' had grown exponentially. She no longer needed to rely on local markets or small online forums. Instead, she had built a thriving business with a loyal customer base that stretched across the country. By cutting out the middlemen, she not only kept her prices competitive but also retained control over her brand's narrative and customer experience.

Ananya's journey from a small home start-up to a well-recognized brand encapsulates the essence of the D2C business model. Let us explore how D2C brands like Pure Radiance are disrupting traditional channels, leveraging technology and customer insights, and paving the way for a new era of consumer engagement and business growth.

Definition of D2C

The D2C business model represents a fundamental shift in how companies interact with and sell to their customers. Traditionally, businesses relied on a series of intermediaries— wholesalers, distributors and retailers—to reach consumers. This chain often resulted in higher costs and less control over the customer experience. D2C businesses, however, sell their products directly to consumers, bypassing these intermediaries and leveraging digital channels to reach their audience. This model often begins with an online-first approach and can expand into omnichannel strategies as the brand grows. Today, we use the D2C business model to describe businesses that initially start off as online only or derive a majority of their revenues from online channels.

Characteristics and Advantages of D2C Business Models

The D2C business model has revolutionized how brands interact with their customers. By bypassing traditional retail channels and selling directly to consumers, D2C brands can maintain better control over the customer experience, gain valuable insights through direct customer data and achieve higher profit margins.

Digital-first Approach

D2C brands typically adopt a digital-first strategy, launching their businesses online before expanding into physical retail spaces. This approach lowers the barrier to entry compared to traditional retail, which requires significant investment in physical stores and distribution networks.

Lenskart: An Indian eyewear brand, Lenskart began as an online retailer, offering a wide range of eyeglasses, contact lenses and sunglasses directly to consumers. The success of their online model allowed them to expand into physical retail, creating an omnichannel presence that enhances customer convenience and satisfaction.

Direct Relationships with Consumers

By selling directly to consumers, D2C brands can build strong, direct relationships with their customers. This direct interaction enables brands to collect valuable data on consumer preferences and behaviours, which can be used to tailor products and marketing efforts.

Mamaearth: This Indian personal care brand engages directly with customers through social media and other digital tools. By gathering feedback and quickly adapting their product offerings, Mamaearth has built a loyal customer base that values the brand's responsiveness and personalization.

Control Over Customer Experience

D2C companies have complete control over the entire customer journey, from the first marketing touchpoint to post-purchase support. This control allows them to ensure a consistent brand message and high-quality service throughout the customer life cycle.

Warby Parker: The global eyewear company offers a home trial programme that allows customers to select frames to try at home. This innovative service enhances convenience and satisfaction, ensuring a positive experience from start to finish.

Higher Profit Margins

By eliminating intermediaries, D2C brands can retain a larger portion of the revenue from each sale. This increased profit margin can be reinvested into marketing, product development and customer service, further strengthening the brand.

Dollar Shave Club: This brand disrupted the traditional razor market by selling directly to consumers through a subscription model. By eliminating retail distribution costs, Dollar Shave Club can offer high-quality razors at competitive prices, while enjoying higher profit margins.

Agility and Innovation

The D2C model allows brands to be more agile and responsive to market trends and consumer feedback. Brands can quickly test new products, gather feedback and make the necessary adjustments, fostering a culture of continuous innovation.

Examples of Successful D2C Brands

BlueStone: BlueStone stands out as a successful D2C jewellery brand in India, utilizing a digital-first strategy combined with an omnichannel presence. Initially launched as an online platform, BlueStone offers over 7,400 jewellery designs with advanced features like 3D rendering to provide an immersive shopping experience. Approximately 90% of its sales are either conducted or influenced online.

Recognizing the high-involvement nature of jewellery purchases, BlueStone expanded to 192 physical stores across 80 cities, seamlessly integrating online and offline channels. Its "Try at Home" service adds another layer of convenience, allowing customers to experience jewellery in their own space. By combining cutting-edge technology with personalized service, BlueStone has transformed the traditional jewellery shopping experience, setting a benchmark for D2C brands.

Nykaa: Nykaa started as an online beauty and wellness retailer and quickly became a household name in India. The brand's digital-first approach allowed it to cater to a tech-savvy customer base, and its expansion into physical stores has solidified its market presence. Nykaa's direct relationships with its customers have enabled it to gather insights and continuously refine its product offerings and marketing strategies.

Mamaearth: Mamaearth has effectively utilized the D2C model to disrupt the personal care industry in India. By focusing on natural and organic products and leveraging social media for marketing and customer engagement, Mamaearth has built a loyal customer base. The brand's ability to respond quickly to customer feedback and trends has been a significant factor in its success.

Casper: Casper revolutionized the mattress industry by selling directly to consumers online. This approach allowed Casper to offer high-quality mattresses at competitive prices, backed by a generous return policy and home delivery service. By controlling the entire customer experience, Casper has maintained a strong brand identity and customer loyalty.

Drivers of the D2C Business Model

The D2C business model has gained significant traction due to several key drivers. These factors have collectively contributed to the growth and success of D2C brands, enabling them to disrupt traditional retail markets and meet the evolving needs of modern consumers.

Unsatisfied and Underserved Consumers

Many consumers find that their specific needs are not adequately addressed by mass-market products. These consumers seek more personalized and unique offerings, which D2C brands are well positioned to provide. By focusing on niche markets, D2C companies can cater to specific demands that are often overlooked by larger, more traditional brands.

Let us look at the Bluestone.com approach. In India's traditional jewellery market, there has been a significant gap in meeting the needs of modern, everyday jewellery consumers. Most traditional brands focus heavily on ornate, wedding-centric jewellery, leaving the growing demand for fashionable, daily wear pieces largely unmet. BlueStone recognized this underserved segment and created a differentiated offering that speaks to contemporary consumer needs.

1. **Focus on Everyday and Contemporary Jewellery**: Unlike conventional jewellers who prioritize wedding and traditional designs, BlueStone offers a wide array of jewellery that caters to daily wear and special occasions. This approach aligns with the growing preference for stylish and trendy jewellery that can be worn daily, especially by the urban, modern demographic.

2. **Technology-Driven Personalization and Convenience**: BlueStone's omnichannel strategy integrates its online and offline presence seamlessly, providing consumers with options such as a 'Try at Home' service and advanced 3D rendering of products. This technology-driven approach ensures that consumers can make informed decisions, feel the products virtually, and experience the convenience of trying jewellery from their homes.

3. **Design Variety and Customization**: With over 7400 designs and regular launches of new collections, BlueStone keeps its product catalogue fresh and aligned with global fashion trends. By continuously analyzing consumer preferences and leveraging data-driven insights, the brand delivers what customers desire, ensuring high satisfaction and engagement.

4. **Addressing Price and Transparency Concerns**: BlueStone provides transparent pricing with detailed breakdowns, including making charges, and certificates of authenticity for gemstones and diamonds. This builds trust among consumers who have traditionally been wary of hidden costs and non-certified jewellery.

Mamaearth recognized a gap in the market for personal care products that are eco-friendly and free of toxins, particularly for mothers and babies. Traditional brands often ignored this niche, focusing instead on broader, mass-market products. By addressing this unmet need, Mamaearth quickly gained a loyal customer base that values natural and safe ingredients.

Dollar Shave Club catered to men who were dissatisfied with the high prices and complex offerings of traditional razor brands. By providing a straightforward, cost-effective subscription service, the company addressed the frustrations of many consumers who felt underserved by existing options.

Convenience and Quick Solutions

Modern consumers prioritize convenience and quick solutions, facilitated by advancements in digital technology. The 'click and get' culture, where products are just a few clicks away, has fuelled the growth of D2C brands. These companies leverage online platforms to offer hassle-free shopping experiences, quick deliveries and easy returns.

Nykaa has capitalized on the demand for convenience by offering a seamless online shopping experience for beauty and wellness products. The brand's easy-to-navigate website and app, coupled with fast delivery and a wide range of products, provide a high level of convenience to its customers.

Casper streamlined the mattress buying process, which traditionally involved visiting multiple stores and dealing with sales pressure. By allowing consumers to purchase mattresses online with the assurance of a generous return policy, Casper made the process significantly more convenient.

Increase in Online Shoppers

The rise in online shopping, particularly among women, has significantly bolstered the D2C market. As more consumers turn to the Internet for their shopping needs, D2C brands have found fertile ground to grow and expand. Women, in particular, represent a substantial and growing segment of online consumers, driving demand for diverse and innovative products.

Lenskart has benefited from the increasing number of online shoppers in India. The brand's online platform offers a wide range of eyewear products, appealing to tech-savvy consumers who prefer the convenience of online shopping. Lenskart's success has been further propelled by its efforts to cater to women's eyewear needs, offering stylish and trendy options.

Sugar Cosmetics is a D2C beauty brand that has effectively tapped into the growing number of female online shoppers. By offering a range of high-quality, affordable make-up products and leveraging social media for marketing, Sugar Cosmetics built a strong following among young, digitally native consumers.

Zivame, an Indian lingerie brand, has successfully leveraged the shift towards online shopping. Recognizing that many women were uncomfortable shopping for lingerie in traditional retail environments, Zivame provided an online platform that offers privacy, convenience and a wide selection of products tailored to various needs.

Emergence of E-commerce Platforms

The emergence of e-commerce platforms has enabled D2C companies to list as sellers and quickly reach consumers online without significant investments or a lengthy gestation period. These platforms provide the infrastructure and audience that D2C brands need to get started and scale their operations efficiently.

Amazon and Flipkart: These major e-commerce platforms have allowed countless D2C brands to access a vast customer base. By listing their products on these platforms, new brands can start selling immediately, leveraging the established logistics, payment systems and customer trust of the platforms.

Etsy: For niche and handmade products, Etsy provides a marketplace where small D2C brands can easily reach a global audience. This platform's built-in audience of buyers looking for unique and personalized products helps new brands gain traction quickly.

Emergence of Third-Party Supportive Ecosystems

The development of a robust third-party ecosystem, including logistics providers, payment gateways and service platforms like Shopify has made it easier for D2C brands to launch and manage their businesses. These services offer essential support functions that were traditionally handled by dealers, distributors, wholesalers and retailers.

Third-party Logistics Providers (3PLs companies like FedEx, DHL and Delhivery) offer comprehensive logistics solutions, including warehousing, packaging and shipping. These services enable D2C brands to manage their supply chain efficiently without investing in their own logistics infrastructure.

Payment Gateways: Services like PhonePe, Stripe and Razorpay provide secure and reliable payment processing, which is crucial for online transactions. These gateways ensure that D2C brands can offer a variety of payment options to their customers, enhancing the shopping experience.

Shopify: This platform offers an all-in-one e-commerce solution, including website building, inventory management and marketing tools. Shopify's ecosystem allows D2C brands to create and manage their online stores with minimal technical expertise, reducing the barrier to entry and enabling quick market launch.

Building a Successful D2C Brand

Creating a strong D2 brand involves several critical elements. These aspects are essential for establishing a solid market presence, building a loyal customer base, and ensuring long-term growth and sustainability.

1. **Strong Brand Identity**

   A compelling brand story and a clear value proposition are vital for standing out in a crowded market. D2C brands need to effectively communicate what makes them unique and why consumers should choose them over competitors. This involves creating a narrative that resonates with the target audience and reflects the brand's values and mission.

   The Souled Store, a pop-culture merchandise brand, has built a strong identity by appealing to young and vibrant audiences who are passionate about TV shows, movies and comics. Their brand story emphasizes creativity, fun, and fandom, making their products instantly relatable to their target audience and creating a strong community of loyal fans.

   BlueStone's brand identity centres around offering modern, customizable jewellery while honouring India's rich heritage in craftsmanship. By blending traditional artistry with contemporary designs, BlueStone appeals to customers looking for elegant yet meaningful jewelry. Their brand story emphasizes trust, quality and accessibility, resonating with customers who value both heritage and innovation.

2. **High-Quality Products**

   Ensuring product quality is non-negotiable for D2C brands aiming to foster customer loyalty. High standards in product development and quality control lead to positive customer experiences, encouraging repeat purchases and word-of-mouth referrals.

BoAt, an Indian audio electronics brand, is known for offering high-quality earphones, headphones and speakers at affordable prices. The brand's commitment to using durable materials and delivering excellent sound quality has helped build a loyal customer base and generate strong word-of-mouth marketing.

Neemli Naturals is an Indian skincare brand known for its high-quality, all-natural products. The brand focuses on using effective and ethically sourced ingredients, ensuring that each product meets the highest quality standards. Neemli Naturals has earned a loyal following by prioritizing product efficacy and safety, backed by scientific research and transparency in ingredient sourcing.

3. **Customer Engagement and Loyalty**

Engaging with customers and building long-term relationships are crucial for a D2C brand's success. Personalized marketing, excellent customer service and loyalty programs can help create meaningful connections with customers.

Bewakoof, a popular Indian fashion brand, engages with its customers through social media campaigns, user-generated content and exclusive offers for loyal customers. The brand's strong online community and creative marketing strategies have helped it build a loyal following.

BlueStone engages customers through personalized shopping experiences, such as the 'Try at Home' service, where customers can see and try jewelry before buying. The brand also offers a loyalty programme that rewards repeat customers, creating incentives for continued engagement. By focusing on excellent customer service and a personalized experience, BlueStone fosters strong, lasting relationships with its clientele.

The Moms Co. engages with its customers by providing personalized content and creating a supportive community for mothers. The brand emphasizes customer feedback and continually adapts its product offerings to meet the needs of moms and babies. Additionally, The Moms Co. has a loyalty programme that rewards repeat customers and encourages referrals, strengthening customer relationships and retention.

4. **Leveraging Social Media and Content Marketing**

Effective use of social media and content marketing can drive brand awareness and engagement. High-quality, relevant content helps educate consumers, build trust and position the brand as an industry authority.

Bombay Shaving Company has effectively used content marketing to engage with its audience, sharing grooming tips, educational content and engaging social media posts. The brand's strategy has helped it connect with its target market and drive conversions.

BlueStone uses social media platforms like Instagram and Facebook to showcase its latest collections, styling tips and behind-the-scenes content. The brand also shares videos and blog content about jewelry trends and craftsmanship, creating an engaging and informative

Wow Skin Science has leveraged social media platforms to create a strong online presence, sharing engaging and informative content about its natural beauty and wellness products. The brand uses content like DIY (Do it Yourself) skincare tips, customer testimonials and behind-the-scenes videos to connect with its audience. By focusing on high-quality, educational content, Wow Skin Science has built a reputation for being a trusted and innovative player in the Indian beauty market.

5. **Influencer Partnerships**

Collaborating with influencers can amplify a brand's reach. Influencers introduce products to new audiences and provide authentic endorsements that help build trust and credibility.

mCaffeine, a personal care brand, has partnered with influencers and celebrities to promote its caffeine-infused skincare products. Leading Bollywood actresses Alia Bhatt, Ileana D'Cruz and Divyanka Tripathi endorse its products and increase its brand awareness. These collaborations have helped the brand reach a wide audience and establish credibility in the beauty and wellness market as a company committed to sustainability and cruelty-free values.

Rage Coffee has strategically partnered with top fitness and lifestyle influencers, including Virat Kohli, Rannvijay Singha and Mumbiker Nikhil, to promote its plant-based, energy-boosting coffee products. By collaborating with influencers who resonate with its health-conscious target demographic, the brand has expanded its reach and bolstered credibility. These partnerships have not only driven brand awareness but also established Rage Coffee as a preferred choice among health-focused coffee lovers.

Logistics and Fulfilment

Logistics and fulfilment are critical components of the D2C model, presenting both challenges and opportunities. Efficient management of these aspects ensures customer satisfaction and operational efficiency, which are vital for the success of any D2C brand.

Inventory Management

Effective inventory management is essential for D2C brands to ensure that products are available when customers want them, minimizing stock-outs and excess inventory. This requires sophisticated demand forecasting and inventory planning.

Nykaa employs advanced inventory management systems to track real-time stock levels across its warehouses and retail stores. By using data analytics, Nykaa can predict demand trends and optimize stock levels, ensuring that popular products are always available while minimizing overstock.

Casper uses sophisticated inventory management techniques to balance production and demand. The company employs a just-in-time inventory system, which minimizes storage costs and reduces the risk of overproduction. This system allows Casper to quickly respond to market demands without maintaining a large inventory.

Shipping and Delivery

Fast and reliable shipping is a key expectation of D2C customers. Brands need to establish efficient logistics networks, often partnering with third-party logistics providers (3PLs) to manage warehousing and delivery.

Lenskart has built a robust logistics network to ensure fast and reliable delivery of eyewear products. The company partners with multiple 3PLs to handle warehousing and shipping, allowing it to offer quick delivery times across India. Lenskart also provides real-time tracking of orders, enhancing the customer experience.

Although not purely D2C, Amazon India sets a benchmark in logistics and delivery. Its extensive network of fulfilment centres and last-mile delivery partners ensures that products reach customers quickly, often within a day or two. This efficiency has set high expectations for D2C brands in terms of delivery speed and reliability.

Warby Parker ensures fast shipping by maintaining regional distribution centres across the United States. These centres allow the company to process and ship orders quickly, often offering customers multiple shipping options, including expedited delivery.

Returns Management

A hassle-free returns process is essential for customer satisfaction. D2C brands need to develop clear and efficient return policies to handle returns and exchanges smoothly.

Casper offers a 100-night trial for its mattresses, allowing customers to return the product if they are not satisfied. This generous return policy is a key part of Casper's customer satisfaction strategy. The company has streamlined its returns process to make it as easy as possible for customers, including free returns and pickups.

Nykaa has a straightforward returns policy that allows customers to return or exchange products within a specified period. The company provides clear instructions on its website and offers customer support to assist with returns, ensuring a smooth process.

Lenskart's return policy includes a fourteen-day no-questions-asked return period. Customers can initiate returns online, and the company provides free return shipping. This policy reduces the risk for customers and encourages them to make purchases with confidence.

Challenges and Risks

Despite its advantages, the D2C model comes with its own set of challenges and risks. These challenges can significantly impact a brand's ability to succeed and grow in the market. Understanding and addressing these challenges is crucial for D2C brands to thrive.

Competition from Established Brands

Established brands with significant resources can pose a serious threat to D2C start-ups. These incumbents can leverage their brand recognition, extensive distribution networks and economies of scale to compete on price and marketing spend.

Casper faced stiff competition from established mattress brands like Serta and Tempur-Pedic. These companies have long-standing reputations and extensive retail networks, allowing them to compete aggressively on price and marketing. To differentiate itself, Casper focused on its unique selling proposition of a simplified buying process, free delivery and a 100-night trial period.

Nykaa, as a D2C beauty brand, competes with well-established cosmetic giants such as L'Oréal and Lakme, that have strong retail presence and brand loyalty. To counter this, Nykaa leveraged its robust online platform, frequent sales and a vast product range to attract and retain customers.

Mamaearth competes with established personal care brands like Johnson & Johnson and Himalaya. These established players have significant market presence and consumer trust. Mamaearth has differentiated itself by focusing on natural and toxin-free products, leveraging influencer marketing and engaging directly with customers through social media.

Changing Consumer Behaviour

Consumer preferences and behaviours are constantly evolving, influenced by technological advancements, economic conditions and cultural trends. D2C brands must stay agile and responsive to these changes to remain relevant.

Warby Parker must continuously adapt to changing fashion trends in eyewear. The brand regularly updates its product line to reflect current styles and preferences, ensuring that it remains appealing to fashion-conscious consumers.

Zivame has had to navigate changing consumer attitudes towards lingerie shopping, particularly the shift towards online purchases driven by privacy concerns and the convenience of home delivery. The brand has responded by enhancing its online shopping experience and providing detailed product information and virtual fitting tools.

High Customer Acquisition Costs

Acquiring new customers can be expensive, especially in competitive markets. D2C brands need to balance spending on acquisition with efforts to retain and nurture existing customers.

Dollar Shave Club initially invested heavily in customer acquisition through viral marketing campaigns, such as its famous launch video. While this strategy helped the brand gain significant traction quickly, maintaining sustainable acquisition costs has been a challenge. The company has since focused on retention strategies, such as subscription services and expanding product lines to improve customer lifetime value.

Casper has faced high customer acquisition costs due to intense competition in the mattress industry. The brand has invested in a mix of online and offline marketing, including podcasts, social media ads and physical showrooms. To mitigate high acquisition costs, Casper has focused on improving customer retention through high-quality products and exceptional customer service.

Lenskart, competing in the highly competitive eyewear market, has faced substantial customer acquisition costs. The brand uses a combination of digital marketing, TV ads and referral programmes to attract new customers. To balance these costs, Lenskart emphasizes customer retention through loyalty programmes, regular eye check-up camps and continuous engagement.

Strategies to Mitigate Challenges

Innovative Marketing and Branding: D2C brands can use creative marketing strategies to stand out from established competitors. For example, leveraging influencer partnerships, social media campaigns and storytelling can build strong brand identity and loyalty.

Agility and Adaptability: Staying agile and responsive to market changes is crucial. This includes continuously monitoring consumer trends, gathering feedback and quickly adapting product offerings and marketing strategies to meet evolving demands.

Focus on Customer Retention: Investing in customer retention can offset high acquisition costs. Building a loyal customer base through personalized marketing, loyalty programmes and excellent customer service can enhance customer lifetime value and improve profitability.

Data-driven Decisions: Utilizing data analytics to understand customer behaviour, preferences and trends can help D2C brands make informed decisions. This data-driven approach can optimize marketing spend, improve retention and derive more lifetime value from customers.

Future of D2C

Technological Innovations

Emerging technologies such as Augmented Reality (AR) and Virtual Reality (VR) are revolutionizing the D2C landscape by providing immersive and interactive experiences that traditional retail cannot match.

BlueStone has embraced these innovations to enhance the online jewellery shopping experience. The brand uses advanced 3D visualization and AR technology to allow customers to virtually try on jewellery pieces from the comfort of their homes. By simply using their smartphones or computers, shoppers can see how a necklace, ring or a pair of earrings will look on them, helping them make informed and confident purchasing decisions. This interactive feature reduces the hesitation often associated with buying expensive jewellery online and minimizes the likelihood of returns. BlueStone's investment in AR exemplifies how D2C brands can use technology to bridge the gap between digital and physical shopping experiences.

Wakefit, a leading Indian D2C brand in the sleep solutions space, has started using AR and VR to help customers visualize how different bed frames, mattresses and home decor items would look in their rooms before making a purchase. By using a mobile app, shoppers can see a 3D representation of their furniture choices, making it easier to select the perfect fit for their home. This use of immersive technology enhances the buying experience and minimizes the uncertainty of purchasing furniture online.

Sustainability and Ethics

Consumer demand for sustainability and ethical practices is growing, and D2C brands that prioritize these values are capturing the attention of environmentally and socially conscious shoppers.

The Better India Shop, an Indian D2C platform, promotes eco-friendly and sustainable products ranging from personal care to household items. The brand partners with local artisans and uses biodegradable materials in its packaging. By supporting fair trade practices and promoting a sustainable lifestyle, The Better India Shop attracts consumers who value ethical sourcing and eco-conscious living.

Thrive Market, a global D2C brand, focuses on providing organic and sustainably sourced grocery items. The company is dedicated to zero-waste packaging and carbon-neutral shipping, resonating with consumers who are increasingly concerned about their environmental impact. Thrive Market also supports ethical farming practices, providing healthy food options while being committed to sustainability and transparency.

Integration of AI and Automation

AI and automation are becoming integral to D2C operations, streamlining processes from marketing to inventory management and improving customer experiences.

Urban Ladder, a prominent Indian furniture brand, uses AI to provide personalized recommendations based on browsing history and user behavior. The brand's AI algorithms suggest furniture styles and designs that match a customer's taste, making the shopping journey more tailored and engaging. Additionally, Urban Ladder uses automated supply chain management to keep inventory optimized, ensuring timely delivery and reducing operational inefficiencies.

Stitch Fix, a global fashion D2C company, uses AI and machine learning to personalize fashion recommendations for its customers. By analyzing data on customer preferences, past purchases and style profiles, Stitch Fix's AI algorithms curate a selection of clothing items that are likely to appeal to individual users. This data-driven approach increases customer satisfaction and reduces the chances of returns, demonstrating how automation and AI can enhance the D2C experience.

The Scalability Challenge and 'House of Brands' Business Model

One of the significant challenges faced by D2C business models is scalability. While many D2C companies start off strong, attracting early adopters and gaining initial traction, they often encounter a growth plateau. This phenomenon, known as 'crossing the chasm,' refers to the difficulty faced in transitioning from early adopters to the mainstream market. Building large companies under the D2C model can be challenging due to several factors such as market saturation, limited customer base and increased competition.

To address these challenges and achieve sustainable growth, D2C companies often adopt two key strategies: diversifying into contiguous and adjacent categories and employing a 'House of Brands' approach.

Diversification into Contiguous and Adjacent Categories

One effective strategy to overcome scalability challenges is diversifying into contiguous and adjacent categories. By expanding their product offerings, D2C brands can tap into new markets and customer segments, thereby driving growth and reducing dependency on a single product line.

Mamaearth started with a focus on baby care products but gradually expanded into personal care products for adults, including skincare, haircare and wellness items. This diversification allowed Mamaearth to reach a broader audience and sustain its growth beyond the initial niche market.

Nykaa began as a beauty and cosmetics retailer but has since diversified into fashion, personal care and wellness products.

By expanding its product range, Nykaa has been able to attract different customer segments and increase its market presence.

Casper initially launched as a mattress company but has since expanded into other sleep-related products such as pillows, bedding and furniture. This approach has helped Casper broaden its appeal and maintain growth momentum.

The House of Brands Approach

Another strategy that D2C companies use to achieve scale is the 'house of brands' approach. This model involves creating or acquiring multiple D2C brands under a single holding company. Each brand operates independently but benefits from shared resources and infrastructure, allowing the parent company to achieve scale through aggregation.

How the Model Works:

1. Brand Acquisition: The holding company acquires existing D2C brands or creates new ones. These brands often cater to different market segments or product categories.
2. Shared Resources: The parent company provides shared resources such as marketing, logistics, technology and customer service. This enables individual brands to operate more efficiently and focus on their core strengths.
3. Cross-promotion: The brands can cross-promote each other, leveraging the customer base of one brand to drive growth for another. This synergy helps in maximizing the overall CLTV.
4. Operational Efficiency: By centralizing certain operations, the holding company can achieve economies of scale, reducing costs and improving profitability across the portfolio of brands.

Examples:

The Indian company, Mensa Brands, follows this strategy. It acquires and scales D2C brands in India, providing them with the resources they need to grow. Mensa Brands focuses on identifying high-potential brands and driving their growth through operational improvements and strategic investments. We will look at this company in more detail.

GOAT Brand Labs, co-founded by Rishi Vasudev, former CEO of Lifestyle International, focuses on acquiring and scaling fashion and lifestyle D2C brands in India. The company provides these brands access to capital, expertise and a robust operational framework, helping them achieve scale and reach new customer segments.

Thrasio is a global example of the house of brands model. It acquires successful Amazon third-party sellers and integrates them into its portfolio. Thrasio leverages its expertise in operations, marketing and supply chain management to scale these brands and enhance their profitability. By aggregating multiple small brands, Thrasio achieved significant scale and market presence before it filed for bankruptcy due to challenges in its business model and a large debt burden.

Key Benefits of House of Brands Model

1. Increased Market Reach: Diversification and multiple brand portfolios enable companies to reach a broader audience and cater to diverse customer needs.
2. Risk Mitigation: Expanding into new categories or operating multiple brands reduces the risk associated with dependence on a single product or market.
3. Operational Synergies: Shared resources and centralized operations improve efficiency and reduce costs, enhancing overall profitability.

4. Enhanced Customer Engagement: Cross-promotion and a wider range of products keep customers engaged and loyal, driving higher lifetime value.

Challenges of House of Brands Model:

1. Integration: Acquiring and integrating new brands or product lines can be complex and requires careful planning and execution.
2. Brand Dilution: Managing multiple brands can dilute the focus and identity of individual brands, if not handled properly.
3. Resource Allocation: Ensuring that each brand or product line receives adequate resources and attention is crucial for maintaining growth across the portfolio.

Mensa Brands Business Model and Company Overview

Mensa Brands is an Indian company that operates under a 'house of brands' business model, focusing on acquiring, scaling and managing digital-first D2C brands. Mensa Brands aims to build a portfolio of high-potential brands across various categories, leveraging its expertise in technology, operations and marketing to drive growth and profitability.

The Mensa Brands business model revolves around the following key components:

1. Acquisition of D2C Brands
   Mensa Brands identifies and acquires established D2C brands that have demonstrated potential but need additional resources and expertise to scale. These brands typically have a strong online presence and a loyal customer base but face challenges in scaling operations, marketing and distribution.
2. Shared Services and Resources

Post-acquisition, Mensa Brands provides its portfolio companies with access to shared services, including:

1. Technology and Data Analytics: Mensa Brands leverages advanced technology and data analytics to optimize various aspects of the business, such as inventory management, demand forecasting and customer insights.
2. Marketing and Branding: The company provides strategic marketing support, including digital marketing, social media campaigns and influencer partnerships, to enhance brand visibility and engagement.
3. Supply Chain and Logistics: Mensa Brands improves operational efficiency by streamlining supply chain and logistics processes, ensuring timely delivery and reducing costs.
4. Financial and Operational Support: The company offers financial backing and operational guidance to help brands scale sustainably and achieve profitability.

As of now, Mensa Brands has acquired several D2C brands across different categories. Some of the notable brands in their portfolio include:

1. Karagiri: A popular D2C brand specializing in traditional Indian sarees and ethnic wear, Karagiri has a strong online presence and caters to customers looking for high-quality, handcrafted ethnic clothing.
2. MyFitness: Known for its range of high-protein peanut butter products, MyFitness targets health-conscious consumers seeking nutritious and delicious food options.
3. Villain: This is a men's grooming and lifestyle brand, offering products such as perfumes, beard care items and accessories. Villain appeals to the modern man who values style and grooming.

4. Florence: This is women's fashion brand, focusing on contemporary and stylish clothing for young women. Florence aims to provide trendy and affordable fashion options for its target audience.

Strengths of Mensa Brands

1. Experienced Leadership: Founder and CEO Ananth Narayanan's extensive experience in e-commerce and retail provides a strong leadership and strategic direction for Mensa Brands. Narayanan's background helps the company navigate the complexities of scaling D2C brands.

2. Technology-driven Approach: Mensa Brands leverages advanced technology and data analytics to optimize business operations, enhance customer experience and drive growth. This tech-driven approach sets the company apart from traditional brand aggregators.

3. Scalable Infrastructure: The company provides a scalable infrastructure that allows acquired brands to benefit from shared services and resources, improving operational efficiency and reducing costs.

4. Diverse Portfolio: By acquiring brands across various categories, Mensa Brands mitigates risk and ensures a diversified revenue stream. This approach also enables cross-promotional opportunities among the brands.

5. Capital Backing: Mensa Brands has secured significant funding from prominent investors, providing the financial resources needed to acquire and scale multiple brands.

Weaknesses of Mensa Brands

1. Integration Challenges: Integrating multiple brands with different operational processes, company cultures and market

strategies can be complex and time-consuming. Mensa Brands must ensure smooth integration to realize synergies.

2. Brand Dilution Risk: Managing a diverse portfolio of brands requires the maintenance of the unique identity and value proposition of each brand. There is a risk of brand dilution, if not managed effectively.

3. Dependence on E-commerce: While the D2C model focuses on digital-first brands, heavy reliance on e-commerce can be a vulnerability. Changes in e-commerce regulations, platform policies or consumer behaviour could impact sales.

4. Market Competition: The D2C space is highly competitive, with many brands vying for consumer attention. Mensa Brands must continuously innovate and adapt to stay ahead of the competition.

5. Scalability Challenges: Scaling multiple brands simultaneously requires significant resources and expertise. Ensuring consistent growth across the portfolio can be challenging, particularly in diverse and dynamic markets.

Summing Up

The D2C business model represents a transformative shift in how companies engage with their customers and operate within the marketplace. By eliminating intermediaries and leveraging digital channels, D2C brands have redefined the consumer experience, providing personalized, convenient and often more affordable products directly to their target audiences. This model's success is fuelled by various drivers, including the rise of online shopping, the demand for unique and personalized products, and the availability of supportive e-commerce platforms and third-party services.

As we have seen through the journeys of brands like Nykaa, Mamaearth, Casper, Warby Parker and Lenskart, the D2C model allows companies to maintain control over their brand narrative, build direct relationships with consumers and rapidly innovate in response to market feedback. The emergence of e-commerce platforms like Amazon, Flipkart and Etsy has further lowered the entry barriers, enabling new D2C brands to reach a broad audience quickly. Additionally, the supportive ecosystem of logistics providers, payment gateways and platforms like Shopify has made it easier than ever for entrepreneurs to launch and scale their businesses.

Looking ahead, the D2C model will continue to evolve, driven by technological advancements such as artificial intelligence, augmented reality and automation. These technologies will enhance the consumer experience, streamline operations and provide deeper insights into customer behaviour. Moreover, as consumers increasingly prioritize sustainability and ethical practices, D2C brands that align with these values will stand out in the marketplace.

8

Pure Digital Business Models: The Creator Economy

A young woman called Misha, in her mid-twenties, works a typical 9 a.m. to 5 p.m. job in a bustling Indian city, but her true passion lies in baking. Even as a child, Ananya loved creating intricate pastries and cakes, dreaming of some day turning her hobby into something more substantial. However, the path to transforming a passion into a viable career often seemed out of reach, dominated as it was by the complexities of traditional business models and the necessity of intermediaries.

One day, while browsing through Instagram, Ananya stumbles upon a series of baking tutorials by a popular food influencer. This influencer, who started sharing her baking journey from a modest kitchen, now boasts millions of followers and collaborates with renowned brands, earning a substantial income from her content. Inspired by this success story, Ananya decides to take a leap of faith.

She starts an Instagram page dedicated to her baking creations, sharing videos and photos of her delightful pastries. Initially, her audience is small—mostly friends and family. But

Ananya remains consistent, posting regularly and engaging with her followers. She begins experimenting with short, engaging videos, and soon, one of her videos goes viral. Overnight, her follower count skyrockets.

With her growing audience, Ananya starts receiving messages from people interested in her recipes and baking techniques. She begins conducting online baking classes, charging a nominal fee. To her surprise, the response is overwhelming. Encouraged by the feedback, Ananya sets up a YouTube channel and a Patreon account, offering exclusive content and personalized baking tips to her subscribers.

As her online presence expands, Ananya catches the eye of several local brands eager to collaborate. She partners with a premium baking supplies company, promoting their products through sponsored content. The additional income allows her to invest in better equipment and ingredients, further enhancing the quality of her creations. Ananya's journey from a passionate hobbyist to a full-fledged content creator is a testament to the transformative power of the Creator Economy.

What Is a Creator Economy?

The Creator Economy refers to a new business model where individuals, referred to as creators, leverage digital platforms to produce and distribute content, monetize their skills, and engage directly with their audience. Unlike traditional business models that rely on intermediaries like publishers, record labels or broadcasters, the Creator Economy empowers individuals to become entrepreneurs, offering their products and services directly to consumers.

Creators can be anyone with a unique skill, passion or expertise, such as writers, artists, musicians, filmmakers, educators and social media influencers. The Creator Economy is built on the foundation of the Internet and digital platforms, which provide creators with the tools to produce, distribute and monetize content at scale. This democratization of content creation has led to a diverse and dynamic ecosystem where niche audiences can find and support the creators they love.

Globally, the Creator Economy has seen exponential growth, driven by platforms like YouTube, Instagram, TikTok and Patreon. For instance, YouTube stars like PewDiePie and TikTok influencers like Charli D'Amelio have built massive followings and lucrative careers by creating engaging content. These platforms provide creators with tools to monetize their content through ads, sponsorships and direct fan support.

In India, the Creator Economy is rapidly expanding, with platforms like YouTube, Instagram and TikTok (before its ban) playing significant roles. Indian creators like Bhuvan Bam (BB Ki Vines) and Prajakta Koli (MostlySane) have amassed millions of followers and diversified their income streams through brand collaborations, merchandise sales and live performances. The rise of regional content and vernacular creators has further fuelled the growth of the Creator Economy in India.

India's Digital Economy and the Rise of the Creator Economy

India's digital economy is a fertile ground for the Creator Economy, characterized by significant data consumption, widespread smartphone usage and the rapid growth of social media platforms. With over 637 million smartphone users and 448 million active social media users, India presents a massive opportunity for creators to reach and engage with audiences.

- Smartphone Penetration: The affordability and accessibility of smartphones have brought millions of Indians online, enabling them to consume and create digital content. Platforms like Jio, which offers inexpensive data plans, have played a crucial role in this digital revolution.
- Social Media Growth: Platforms such as Instagram, YouTube and TikTok (before its ban) have seen exponential growth in India.

The convergence of high smartphone penetration, affordable data and social media proliferation has created an environment ripe for the Creator Economy. Creators can reach vast audiences without the need for traditional media channels, and consumers have unprecedented access to a diverse array of content. This democratization of media has not only amplified individual voices but also fostered innovation in content creation and monetization strategies.

Types of Creators

The Creator Economy encompasses a diverse range of creators, each leveraging their unique skills and platforms to generate revenue. Here are some prominent types:

Bloggers

Bloggers create written content on various topics, from lifestyle and travel to technology and finance. They monetize their blogs through advertising, sponsored posts and affiliate marketing. For example, Indian blogger Shradha Sharma of YourStory has built a successful platform that features stories of entrepreneurs and start-ups, generating revenue through ads and sponsored content.

YouTubers

YouTubers create video content on platforms like YouTube, covering niches such as gaming, education, beauty and vlogging. They earn money through ad revenue, brand deals and merchandise sales. Global examples include MrBeast, known for his philanthropic stunts, and Indian YouTuber CarryMinati, famous for his comedic and roast videos.

Podcasters

Podcasters produce audio content on various subjects, often monetizing through sponsorships, listener donations and premium content. Joe Rogan's podcast, 'The Joe Rogan Experience,' is a global success, while Indian podcasters like Amit Varma of 'The Seen and the Unseen' have gained a significant following.

Social Media Influencers

Influencers leverage platforms like Instagram, TikTok and Twitter to create content and engage with their followers. They monetize through sponsored posts, affiliate marketing and brand partnerships. Influencers like Kylie Jenner and Indian fashion influencer Komal Pandey exemplify this category.

Artists

Artists, including musicians, painters and digital creators, use platforms like Spotify, Etsy and Behance to showcase and sell their work. They earn through direct sales, streaming revenue and fan support. Indian artist Raghava K.K., known for his digital art, has successfully monetized his creations through various digital platforms.

Creator's Business Life Cycle

The lifecycle of a creator's business can be split into 4 segments:

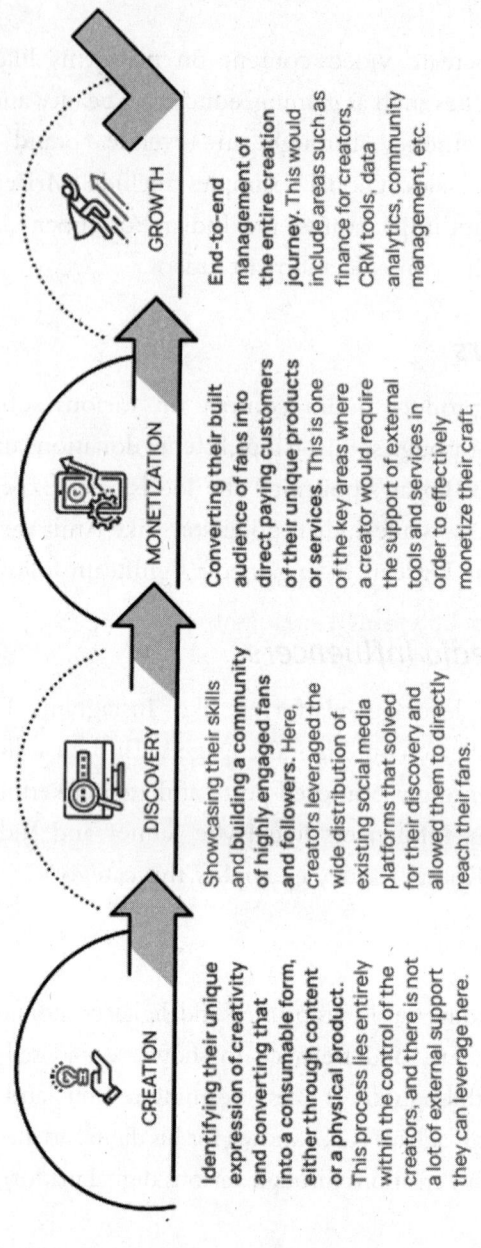

CREATION

Identifying their unique expression of creativity and converting that into a consumable form, either through content or a physical product. This process lies entirely within the control of the creators, and there is not a lot of external support they can leverage here.

DISCOVERY

Showcasing their skills and building a community of highly engaged fans and followers. Here, creators leveraged the wide distribution of existing social media platforms that solved for their discovery and allowed them to directly reach their fans.

MONETIZATION

Converting their built audience of fans into direct paying customers of their unique products or services. This is one of the key areas where a creator would require the support of external tools and services in order to effectively monetize their craft.

GROWTH

End-to-end management of the entire creation journey. This would include areas such as finance for creators, CRM tools, data analytics, community management, etc.

Source: Creator Economy–A Kalaari Capital report [1]

---

[1] 'Creator Economy', *Kalaari Capital*, January 2022, https://www.kalaari.com/wp-content/uploads/2022/01/Creator-Economy-Kalaari-Capital.pdf

Drivers for the Growth of the Creator Economy

The Creator Economy has seen remarkable growth driven by several fundamental changes in consumer behaviour and macroeconomic factors.

Emphasis on Individuality and Authenticity

Consumers today increasingly value authenticity and individuality in the content and products they consume. Unlike the mass-produced content of traditional media, the Creator Economy allows individuals to express their unique perspectives and experiences, resonating more deeply with audiences who seek genuine connections.

YouTube Creators: The success of YouTubers like Casey Neistat and Lilly Singh highlights this shift. Neistat's vlogs are celebrated for their raw, unfiltered storytelling, while Singh's content reflects her authentic voice and personal experiences, building a strong rapport with her audience.

Local Influencers: In India, influencers like Prajakta Koli (MostlySane) create content that is relatable to the everyday life of young Indians, from addressing social issues to sharing personal stories, which resonates deeply with their audience.

The emphasis on individuality and authenticity has reshaped marketing strategies. Brands are now partnering with creators who align with their values, as consumers are more likely to trust and engage with recommendations from authentic sources. This shift is also evident in the rise of niche markets where creators cater to specific interests, fostering a more diverse and inclusive digital landscape.

Reduced Attention Spans

Modern consumers have reduced attention spans, leading to the rise of bite-sized, instantly gratifying content. Platforms like TikTok, Instagram Reels and Twitter have capitalized on this trend by providing short-form content that captures attention quickly.

- TikTok: This platform's format of fifteen- to sixty-second videos has become immensely popular, allowing creators to deliver impactful messages in a short time. Viral challenges, dance routines and comedic skits are prime examples of how brief content can engage large audiences.
- Instagram Reels: Similar to TikTok, Instagram Reels allows users to create and discover short, engaging videos, fostering creativity and immediate engagement.

This trend has significant implications for content creation and consumption. Creators need to be more innovative and concise in their messaging, while platforms continuously optimize algorithms to surface the most engaging content. Brands also adapt by creating short, impactful advertisements that fit seamlessly into these platforms, maximizing their reach and effectiveness.

Desire for Self-curated Content

Consumers now prefer to curate the type of content they consume rather than relying on third-party distributors. This self-curation is facilitated by algorithms and personalized recommendations on digital platforms, empowering users to build their own media experiences.

- Spotify Playlists: Users create and share their own playlists, customizing their music experience to fit their tastes and moods. Spotify's Discover Weekly and Daily Mix playlists use algorithms to suggest songs based on listening habits, further personalizing the user experience.
- YouTube Subscriptions: Users subscribe to channels that align with their interests, from cooking tutorials and fitness videos to educational content and vlogs, creating a personalized content feed.

The move towards self-curated content reflects a broader shift in control from producers to consumers. This democratization of content consumption has led to the proliferation of diverse voices and perspectives, as users can easily find and follow creators who match their interests. Platforms benefit by enhancing user satisfaction and engagement through personalized experiences.

Strong Community Bonds

There is a growing desire among consumers to form strong communities, even in niche segments. These communities provide a sense of belonging and shared purpose, often centred around specific interests or identities.

- Facebook Groups: Facebook groups serve as hubs for communities to connect over shared interests, whether it's a local hiking club, a book discussion group or a professional networking forum.
- Reddit Communities: Subreddits like r/fitness, r/gaming and r/India offer spaces where users can discuss topics, share experiences and provide support, fostering a sense of community among members.

Strong community bonds enhance engagement and loyalty, as members feel a deeper connection with both the community and its leaders. For creators, building a dedicated community can lead to more consistent support and monetization opportunities, such as through Patreon memberships or exclusive content offerings. Brands also leverage these communities to build deeper relationships with their target audiences, using insights gathered from community interactions to tailor their marketing strategies.

Platforms in the Creator Economy

Various digital platforms play a crucial role in the Creator Economy by providing creators with the tools and audience they need to monetize their content.

YouTube:

YouTube allows creators to upload videos and earn through ad revenue, memberships and super chats.

Pros: Large audience, multiple monetization options.

Cons: High competition, reliance on YouTube's algorithm.

MrBeast, a YouTube creator known for his extravagant challenges and philanthropy, earns millions through ads, sponsorships and merchandise.

Technical Guruji, a tech review channel by Gaurav Chaudhary, generates substantial income through ad revenue and brand collaborations.

Instagram:

Instagram provides creators with a platform to share photos and videos, earning through sponsored posts, affiliate marketing and Instagram TV ads.

Pros: High engagement, visual platform.

Cons: Algorithm changes, limited direct monetization options, compared to other platforms.

Huda Kattan, a beauty influencer and entrepreneur, leverages her massive Instagram following to promote her cosmetics brand, Huda Beauty.

Komal Pandey uses Instagram to showcase her fashion sense and collaborates with brands for sponsored posts.

TikTok:

TikTok enables creators to share short-form videos, earning through brand partnerships, sponsored content and the Creator Fund.

Pros: Viral potential, large and engaged user base.

Cons: Unpredictable algorithm, recent scrutiny and regulatory challenges.

Charli D'Amelio, a TikTok star, earns through sponsorships, her own merchandise and brand collaborations.

Riyaz Aly, a popular TikTok influencer, monetized his fame through brand partnerships and promotional videos before TikTok was banned in India.

Patreon:

Patreon allows creators to receive ongoing financial support from their fans in exchange for exclusive content and perks.

Pros: Stable income, direct fan engagement.

Cons: Requires consistent content creation, platform fees.

Podcaster Sam Harris uses Patreon to offer bonus content and early access episodes to his subscribers.

Indian comic book artist Abhijeet Kini uses Patreon to fund his projects and provide exclusive artwork to his supporters.

Key Opportunity Areas

The Creator Economy is supported by several platforms and companies that significantly enhance the capabilities and revenue potential for creators. The business model of these companies benefits from the growth of the Creator Economy and thrives as more creators join the platforms. Let us look at some of these.

Direct Monetization Platforms

Direct monetization platforms enable creators to offer direct fan subscriptions, exclusive content, one-on-one communication, tipping and donations. These platforms allow creators to monetize their audience directly without relying on traditional advertising or sponsorships.

Patreon: Patreon allows creators to earn a sustainable income by offering memberships to their fans. Creators offer various tiers of subscriptions that provide exclusive content, early access or special perks. Musicians, podcasters and artists worldwide use Patreon to connect with their fans and generate revenue.

YouTube Memberships: YouTube offers a membership feature where viewers can subscribe to their favourite channels for a monthly fee in exchange for exclusive content, badges and emojis. This feature is widely used by content creators across different genres.

Buy Me a Coffee: This platform allows creators to receive tips and donations from their audience. Creators can set up a profile and share their work, encouraging fans to support them with small monetary contributions.

Creator-led Commerce

Creator-led commerce platforms facilitate influencer-driven user acquisition and live commerce, allowing creators to sell products directly to their audience.

Shopify: Shopify enables creators to set up their online stores and sell products directly to their audience. Many influencers and creators use Shopify to sell merchandise, digital products and more.

Myntra Studio: Myntra, an Indian e-commerce platform, launched Myntra Studio, where fashion influencers and creators can showcase their styles and promote products directly. This feature integrates content with commerce, driving sales through influencer endorsements.

Meesho: A social commerce platform, Meesho allows individuals to resell products through social media platforms like WhatsApp and Facebook. Many creators use Meesho to curate and sell products to their followers.

Creator Tools

Creator tools are essential for managing, building and growing a creator's business. These include CRM tools, data analytics, legal work, web builders and more.

Canva: Canva is a graphic design tool that helps creators design engaging visuals for their content. It provides templates and easy-to-use design tools, making it accessible to creators without a design background.

Hootsuite: Hootsuite is a social media management tool that helps creators schedule posts, analyse performance and manage multiple social media accounts from one dashboard.

Dukaan: Dukaan helps small business owners and creators set up online stores quickly. It provides tools for managing inventory, processing payments and tracking orders.

NFTs and Social Tokens

Here are some platforms that open new monetization channels for creators through the rise of Non-Fungible Tokens (NFT) and social tokens.

OpenSea (Global): OpenSea is one of the largest NFT marketplaces where artists and creators can mint, sell and auction their digital assets. Many artists have successfully monetized their digital art through NFTs on OpenSea.

Full Stack Platforms

Full Stack platforms help creators in specific niches, such as health, fitness, beauty, dance and music, to bring their services online and scale their businesses.

ClassPass: It is a platform for fitness and wellness creators to offer their classes online. Creators can reach a global audience, offering live and on-demand sessions.

Udemy (Global): It is an online learning platform where educators and experts can create and sell courses. It allows creators to monetize their knowledge and reach a wide audience.

FITTR: It is an Indian platform where fitness coaches can offer personalized training and nutrition plans. It provides tools for managing clients, tracking progress and building a fitness community.

Community Management

These are platforms that help creators build strong, engaged communities with greater peer-to-peer interaction and knowledge sharing.

Discord (Global): Discord provides servers where creators can build communities around their interests. It supports text, voice and video communication, making it a versatile tool for community engagement.

Circle: A community platform that allows creators to build membership-based communities. It integrates with other tools like Zoom and Slack to facilitate interactions and content sharing. Creators receive financial support directly from their audience through platforms like Patreon, Ko-fi, and Buy Me a Coffee. Due to the direct support from fans, this fosters a strong community build-up. However, the revenue can be inconsistent and so a very large and loyal fan base is needed for the amount to be significant.

Amanda Palmer, a musician and artist, relies on Patreon to fund her creative projects, receiving support from her fans directly.

Influencer Marketing

Influencer marketing is a powerful marketing method where brands collaborate with influencers to promote their products or services. This approach has gained immense popularity due to the unique trust and engagement that influencers have with their audiences. Unlike traditional advertising, influencer marketing leverages the personal connections influencers build with their followers, creating authentic and relatable promotional content.

Influencer marketing involves a strategic partnership between brands and influencers, individuals who have established credibility and a substantial following in specific niches. These influencers use their platforms to share content that promotes the brand's products in a way that feels organic and genuine. The personal connection influencers have with their followers makes the promotional content more impactful, often resulting in higher engagement rates and better conversion compared to traditional advertising methods.

Brands typically start by identifying influencers whose audience aligns with their target market. Once these influencers are identified, they collaborate with them to create content that highlights their products or services in an engaging and authentic manner. The content is then shared on the influencer's platform, whether it be Instagram, YouTube, TikTok or another social media site, reaching a broad and engaged audience.

For example, Nike frequently collaborates with athletes and fitness influencers to promote its products. These influencers create compelling content that resonates with fitness enthusiasts, showcasing Nike's apparel and gear in action. Similarly, Mamaearth partners with numerous beauty influencers to promote its natural and eco-friendly products, leveraging the influencers' reach to tap into a wider audience.

Key Players

Influencer marketing involves several key players:

1. Influencers: Individuals who create content and have a substantial following.
2. Brands: Companies looking to promote their products or services.
3. Audience: Followers of the influencers who consume the content and may be influenced by their recommendations.
4. Platforms: Social media sites like Instagram, YouTube, TikTok and others where influencers share content.

Top Influencers in India

1. Virat Kohli
   • Platform: Instagram
   • Followers: 265.7 million

- Brands: Promoted brands include Blue Star, Well Man, Himalaya, Myntra, Google Duo, Mobile Premier League, Puma, Hero MotoCorp, etc.

2. Prajakta Koli
   - Platform: Instagram, YouTube
   - Followers: 8 million on Instagram
   - Brands: Various brand endorsements through her comedic and lifestyle content.

3. Bhuvan Bam
   - Platform: Instagram, YouTube
   - Followers: 18.4 million on Instagram
   - Brands: Multiple brand collaborations through his comedic sketches and music.

4. Jannat Zubair Rahmani
   - Platform: Instagram
   - Followers: 45.1 million
   - Brands: UBON and various endorsements in fashion, beauty and lifestyle sectors.

5. Komal Pandey
   - Platform: Instagram, YouTube
   - Followers: 1.9 million on Instagram
   - Brands: Whisper, Vaseline, Myntra, Google, and other fashion and beauty brands.

Top Global Influencers

1. Cristiano Ronaldo
   - Platform: Instagram
   - Followers: 626 million
   - Brands: Nike, Armani, Clear, Herbalife, Livescore and Tag Heuer. Earns approximately $3.23 million per post.

2. Kylie Jenner
   - Platform: Instagram
   - Followers: 399 million
   - Brands: Kylie Cosmetics, Balmain and other high-end fashion brands. Earns around $1.84 million per post.
3. Selena Gomez
   - Platform: Instagram
   - Followers: 429 million
   - Brands: Coca-Cola, Louis Vuitton, Puma, Verizon, Rare Beauty and Pantene. Earns approximately $2.5 million per post.
4. Dwayne Johnson (The Rock)
   - Platform: Instagram
   - Followers: 395 million
   - Brands: Under Armour, Voss Water, Project Rock and various movie promotions. Earns around $1.71 million per post.
5. Lionel Messi
   - Platform: Instagram
   - Followers: 500 million
   - Brands: Adidas, Budweiser, Gatorade, Huawei, Pepsi, Lay's and Mastercard. Earns approximately $2.6 million per post.

These influencers leverage their massive followings to promote a variety of brands, significantly impacting consumer behaviour and brand visibility. By creating authentic and engaging content, influencers bridge the gap between brands and consumers, fostering a more personal connection that traditional advertising often lacks.

Challenges in the Creator Economy

Despite the opportunities, creators face several challenges that can impact their ability to build and sustain their businesses.

Copyright Infringement:

Creators often deal with issues related to unauthorized use of their content, which can result in lost revenue and legal complications. YouTube creators frequently face copyright claims from music companies, even for background music used in their videos. Indian YouTubers and content creators often have their videos taken down or demonetized due to copyright issues related to music and video clips.

Algorithm Changes:

Digital platforms frequently update their algorithms, which can drastically affect a creator's reach and revenue.

Instagram's algorithm changes have often led to reduced visibility for many influencers, affecting their engagement and income. Changes in YouTube's algorithm have impacted Indian creators like technical educators, leading to fluctuations in video views and ad revenue.

Platform Policies:

Creators must navigate complex platform policies that can affect their content and monetization strategies.

YouTube's stringent community guidelines have led to demonetization for creators discussing sensitive topics. TikTok's ban in India forced many creators to shift to other platforms, disrupting their content creation and revenue streams.

Monetization and Payment Issues:

Fluctuating ad rates, payment delays and platform fees can impact a creator's income stability.

YouTube's fluctuating CPM (cost per thousand impressions) rates can lead to unpredictable ad revenue for creators. Indian creators on international platforms like Patreon may face issues with payment processing and currency conversion fees.

Mental Health and Burnout:

The pressure to consistently produce engaging content can lead to burnout and mental health challenges for creators. Many YouTubers and social media influencers have spoken openly about the mental health challenges and burnout caused by the demand for regular content and audience engagement.

Monetization Strategies

Creators employ various monetization strategies to generate income from their content.

Sponsored Content

Creators collaborate with brands to create content that promotes the brand's products or services. This can include social media posts, videos, blog articles and podcasts.

This builds long-term relationships with brands, leading to potentially high revenue, but requires a large audience to attract brands, and can create trust issues with the audience, if not done authentically.

YouTuber Marques Brownlee (MKBHD) frequently collaborates with tech companies to review and promote their latest gadgets. Fashion blogger Masoom Minawala partners with various fashion brands such as L'Oréal, Louis Vuitton, H&M, etc. to showcase their products on her Instagram account

Affiliate Marketing

Creators earn commissions by promoting products or services and driving sales through affiliate links. This strategy is popular among bloggers and YouTubers who review or recommend products. While this provides passive income and can scale as the number of followers increases, it works only if there is a large audience, and the fans actually buy the product using the affiliate link.

Pat Flynn of Smart Passive Income generates significant revenue through affiliate marketing by promoting tools and resources for entrepreneurs. Blogger Ankit Singla of 'Master Blogging' earns through affiliate marketing by recommending blogging tools and services.

Merchandise Sales

Creators design and sell their own branded merchandise, such as clothing, accessories or digital products. Platforms like Shopify and Teespring facilitate this process. The creators can price the items at their discretion, the profit margins are normally high and can develop and maintain a strong brand identity. However, it requires upfront investment, and there may be inventory management challenges.

YouTubers Rhett and Link from Good Mythical Morning sell branded merchandise through their online store. Bhuvan Bam sells BB Ki Vines branded merchandise, including T-shirts and accessories, to his fan base.

Fan Donations

Creators receive financial support from their fans through platforms like Patreon, Buy Me a Coffee and YouTube memberships. This model is popular among podcasters, artists and niche content creators. This enables direct revenue generation from fans without needing any third-party involvement. On the other hand, it can be unpredictable. This stream needs a very large loyal fan base for the amounts to be meaningful.

Kanan Gill, an Indian stand-up comedian and content creator, utilizes platforms like Buy Me a Coffee and Patreon to receive support from his fans. Known for his comedy sketches and YouTube series, Gill offers his patrons behind-the-scenes content, exclusive videos and other perks in exchange for their support.

Influencer Platforms Monetization

Various platforms have emerged to support and facilitate the Creator Economy, each offering unique tools and opportunities for creators to monetize their content.

Instagram

Instagram offers monetization options like sponsored posts, affiliate marketing and Instagram Shops. Indian fashion influencers like Masoom Minawala use Instagram to collaborate with brands and sell their own products.

YouTube

YouTube provides creators with multiple revenue streams, including ad revenue, channel memberships and Super Chat.

Global creators like Marques Brownlee (MKBHD) and Indian YouTuber Technical Guruji have built successful careers on YouTube.

TikTok

TikTok, a short-form video platform, has gained immense popularity. Creators monetize through brand partnerships, live gifts and the TikTok Creator Fund. Despite its ban in India, TikTok influencers like Riyaz Aly had amassed millions of followers and lucrative brand deals.

Patreon

Patreon allows creators to receive recurring payments from their fans in exchange for exclusive content and perks. This platform is popular among podcasters, artists and niche content creators. Indian musician Ankur Tewari uses Patreon to offer exclusive music and behind-the-scenes content to his supporters.

Key Success Metrics for Start-ups in the Creator Economy

Start-ups in the Creator Economy employ various business models, such as SaaS for creator tools, direct fan subscriptions, creator commerce, creator aggregation and brand collaborations. Tracking specific key metrics is crucial to gauge their success and sustainability. Here's an in-depth look at these metrics, their definitions and examples to illustrate their importance.

Conversion of Audience to Paid Subscribers

The conversion rate of audience to paid subscribers measures the percentage of a creator's audience that transitions from free followers to paying customers. This metric signifies how effectively a platform or a creator can monetize their audience.

A high conversion rate indicates that the content or value proposition is compelling enough to encourage followers to pay for premium access. This is critical for platforms offering direct fan subscriptions, as it directly impacts revenue. Monitoring this metric helps creators and platforms understand the effectiveness of their monetization strategies and make necessary adjustments to improve their offerings.

Recurring Revenue for Creator Tools

In the Creator Economy, a wide array of tools is available to help creators build and manage their businesses. These tools span various categories, including content creation, monetization, project management and audience engagement. The companies that make these tools offer them typically on a subscription basis to creators in the SaaS business model. They track metrics such as Monthly Recurring Revenue (MRR), Annual Recurring Revenue (ARR), CAC, and CLTV.

Recurring revenue metrics are vital for understanding the financial health and growth potential of SaaS platforms. MRR and ARR provide insights into predictable revenue streams, while CAC and CLTV help evaluate the cost-effectiveness of customer acquisition and the long-term value generated from each customer. A high CLTV, relative to CAC, indicates a sustainable business model with efficient customer acquisition and retention strategies.

Creator Earnings

Tracking the earnings of creators on a platform involves monitoring the revenue generated by creators through various monetization channels. This metric is essential as it correlates with creator satisfaction, platform loyalty and reduced churn.

Higher creator earnings signify that the platform is effectively facilitating monetization opportunities, leading to greater creator satisfaction and retention. Platforms must ensure that a significant portion of creators can earn a sustainable income to maintain loyalty and reduce churn rates. This metric also helps platforms identify the most profitable and engaging content or monetization strategies.

User Growth and Engagement Metrics

User growth measures the increase in the number of users on a platform over a specific period. Engagement metrics, including likes, comments, shares and active usage rates, measure how actively users interact with the platform and its content.

Continuous user growth indicates that the platform is attracting new users, which is crucial for scalability. High engagement rates reflect the platform's ability to retain users and encourage interaction, leading to a more vibrant and active community. For community-driven platforms, these metrics are crucial as they directly impact monetization opportunities and overall platform success. High engagement rates often lead to higher retention and conversion rates, as engaged users are more likely to become paying customers.

Impact of Generative AI on the Creator Economy

The advent of Generative AI has brought profound changes to various industries, and the Creator Economy is no exception. By leveraging machine learning algorithms to generate content, these AI systems can create text, images, music and videos, thereby transforming how content is produced and consumed.

Positive Impacts of Generative AI

1. Enhanced Creativity and Productivity:
    Generative AI tools can significantly boost the productivity of creators by automating repetitive tasks and providing creative suggestions. For instance, AI-powered writing assistants like OpenAI's GPT-4 can help writers generate ideas, draft articles and even edit content. Similarly, visual artists can use AI tools to generate preliminary sketches or enhance their digital artwork.

    *   Jasper.ai: This AI writing assistant helps content creators generate blog posts, social media updates and marketing copy. By automating the initial draft creation, Jasper.ai allows creators to focus on refining and personalizing their content.

    *   DALL-E: OpenAI's DALL-E generates images from textual descriptions, enabling artists to visualize concepts quickly and iterate on designs more efficiently.

2. Democratization of Content Creation:
    Generative AI lowers the barriers to entry for aspiring creators who may lack advanced technical skills. By providing accessible tools that simplify content creation, AI empowers more people to participate in the Creator Economy.

    *   Canva's AI Features: Canva integrates AI tools that help users create professional-quality graphics without needing advanced design skills. Features like Magic Resize and Auto Enhance make it easier for everyone to produce visually appealing content.

3. Personalized Content for Audiences:
    AI algorithms can analyse user preferences and generate personalized content recommendations, enhancing user engagement and satisfaction. This capability is particularly

valuable for platforms that host a vast amount of user-generated content.

- YouTube's Recommendation Algorithm: YouTube uses AI to recommend videos tailored to individual user preferences, helping creators reach their target audiences more effectively.

4. Scalable Content Production:

AI-generated content can be produced at scale, allowing creators to maintain a consistent presence across multiple platforms. This scalability is crucial for staying relevant in the fast-paced digital landscape.

- Lumen5: This is a video creation platform that uses AI to transform blog posts into engaging videos, enabling creators to repurpose their written content and reach wider audiences on video-centric platforms like YouTube and TikTok.

Negative Impacts of Generative AI

1. Quality and Originality Concerns:

While Generative AI can produce large volumes of content, there are concerns about the quality and originality of AI-generated works. AI-generated content might lack the nuanced understanding and emotional depth that human creators bring to their work.

- AI-Generated Music: While tools like OpenAI's MuseNet can compose music, critics argue that AI-generated compositions often lack the emotional resonance and creativity of human-made music.

2. Job Displacement:

As AI automates various aspects of content creation, there is a risk of job displacement for professionals whose tasks can be replicated by AI. Writers, graphic designers and video editors may face increased competition from AI tools that can perform similar functions more efficiently.

- Freelance Writers: Platforms like ContentBot offer AI writing services that can produce articles and blog posts, potentially reducing demand for freelance writers.

3. Ethical and Copyright Issues:
    The use of AI in content creation raises ethical and copyright concerns. AI systems trained on existing content may inadvertently reproduce copyrighted material, leading to legal disputes.

    - AI Art Generators: Some AI art generators have faced backlash for creating works that closely resemble existing copyrighted images, raising questions about intellectual property rights and originality.

4. Dependence on Technology:
    An over-reliance on AI tools can lead to a homogenization of content, where distinct creative voices are overshadowed by algorithmically generated works. This dependence might also stifle innovation and the development of unique artistic styles.

    - Social Media Influencers: Influencers using AI tools to automate content creation might produce posts that lack authenticity and personal touch, potentially diminishing audience trust and engagement.

Who Benefits and Who Loses?

Beneficiaries:

1. Aspiring Creators:
    Individuals with limited technical skills benefit from AI tools that simplify content creation, allowing them to enter the Creator Economy more easily.

- Example: Canva users can create professional-quality designs without prior graphic design experience.

2. Established Creators:
   Established creators can use AI to enhance their productivity and expand their content repertoire, maintaining a competitive edge in a crowded market.
   - Example: YouTubers leveraging AI tools for video editing and SEO optimization can streamline their workflows and increase their output.

3. Content Platforms:
   Platforms that integrate AI-driven features can offer more personalized and engaging user experiences, attracting and retaining more users.
   - Example: Spotify uses AI to curate personalized playlists, enhancing user satisfaction and engagement.

Potential Losers:

1. Traditional Content Creators:
   As mentioned earlier, professionals in fields like writing, graphic design and video editing may face job displacement or reduced demand as AI tools become more prevalent.
   - Example: Freelance writers competing with AI writing services might find it challenging to secure work.

2. Audiences:
   Consumers might experience content fatigue from the proliferation of AI-generated content, which can lack the authenticity and originality of human-created works.
   - Example: Social media users inundated with AI-generated posts may become disengaged if the content feels repetitive or impersonal.

3. Small Platforms:
    Smaller content platforms without the resources to invest in
    advanced AI technologies may struggle to compete with larger
    platforms that offer superior AI-driven user experiences.
    -   Example: Niche content sites might lose users to
        major platforms like YouTube and Instagram, which
        provide more personalized content recommendations
        through AI.

Generative AI is a double-edged sword in the Creator Economy.
As the Creator Economy continues to evolve, it will be essential
to balance the benefits of AI with the need to preserve human
creativity and authenticity.

The Creator Economy is poised for significant growth,
driven by the increasing number of creators and the evolving
digital landscape. As monetization models mature, millions
of creators and knowledge professionals will pursue micro-
entrepreneurship, benefiting from rising consumer spending and
India's growing GDP. Consumers will continue to support their
favourite creators, fostering deeper relationships powered by an
ecosystem of tools and platforms that enable this shift.

Key Takeaways

1. Empowerment Through Digital Platforms:
    -   Digital platforms enable individuals to turn their passions
        into their careers.
    -   Tools like Instagram, YouTube and Patreon democratize
        content creation and monetization.
2. The Rise and Impact of the Creator Economy:
    -   Shifts from traditional models by connecting creators
        directly with audiences.

- Significant growth fuelled by high smartphone penetration and social media.
- Examples: Indian creators Bhuvan Bam and Prajakta Koli.

3. Diverse Range of Creators:
   - Includes bloggers, YouTubers, podcasters, social media influencers and artists.
   - Different monetization strategies such as advertising, affiliate marketing and brand deals.

4. Key Drivers of Growth:
   - Individuality and Authenticity: Consumers prefer genuine, relatable content.
   - Reduced Attention Spans: Platforms like TikTok cater to quick, impactful messages.
   - Self-curated Content: Algorithms empower users to customize their content experiences.
   - Strong Community Bonds: Digital platforms facilitate engaged communities.

5. Monetization Strategies:
   - Sponsored Content: Brand collaborations.
   - Affiliate Marketing: Commissions from product promotions.
   - Merchandise Sales: Selling branded products.
   - Fan Donations: Financial support from fans through Patreon, Buy Me a Coffee, etc
   - Platform-specific Monetization: YouTube, Instagram or TikTok features.

6. Challenges in the Creator Economy:
   - Copyright Infringement: Unauthorized use of content.
   - Algorithm Changes: Impact on reach and revenue.
   - Platform Policies: Navigating complex, changing rules.

- Monetization and Payment Issues: Ad rate fluctuations, payment delays.
- Mental Health and Burnout: Pressure to produce engaging content.

7. Impact of Generative AI:
   - Positive Impacts: Boosts creativity/productivity, democratizes creation and personalizes content.
   - Negative Impacts: Quality concerns, job displacement, ethical issues and dependence on tech.

8. Beneficiaries and Potential Losers:
   - Beneficiaries: Aspiring and established creators and content platforms.
   - Potential Losers: Traditional content creators, smaller platforms and audiences facing content fatigue.

9

Business Models Around Digital Public Goods and Digital Public Infrastructure

Introduction

Imagine a bustling marketplace in a small Indian town, where local artisans showcase their handcrafted goods, farmers sell fresh produce, and small shop owners cater to the daily needs of the community. Now, envision this vibrant market extending its reach far beyond its geographic confines, connecting sellers with buyers from across the country, and even the world, through the power of digital technology. This is not a distant dream, but reality made possible thanks to Digital Public Goods (DPGs) and Digital Public Infrastructure (DPI).

Consider the case of Ramesh, a small business owner in a rural part of India. Ramesh's family has been producing high-quality handmade textiles for generations, but their market was limited to the towns nearby. With the advent of India Stack and platforms like ONDC, Ramesh can now list his products online, reaching a vast customer base without needing any expensive intermediaries. Through UPI, he seamlessly receives payments, and with DigiLocker, he securely stores and shares important business documents. Ramesh's business has not only survived but thrived, growing beyond local borders to serve a national and even international clientele. (While listing on platforms like Amazon or Flipkart is a possibility, it comes with significant barriers for small sellers like Ramesh. These platforms often charge high commissions and impose strict terms, making it difficult for local artisans to compete or maintain fair profit margins. Additionally, sellers have limited control over customer data and must adhere to the platform's rules, which can restrict their business flexibility and growth potential.)

This chapter explores the transformative power of DPGs and DPI, with a special focus on how these innovations have enabled SMEs, start-ups and local businesses to flourish. From the Linux operating system to India's Aadhaar, UPI and ONDC initiatives, we delve into the mechanisms by which digital public goods democratize access to technology, promote economic growth and foster inclusive development.

Digital Public Goods

In the digital age, the traditional barriers of geography and scale are being dismantled, creating a more equitable playing field for businesses of all sizes. As we journey through the landscape of Digital Public Goods and Infrastructure, we will uncover the strategies and tools that are not only driving economic transformation but also shaping the future of global commerce.

DPGs represent a transformative approach to the distribution of resources and services in the digital age. Unlike traditional public goods such as roads, libraries and parks, which are tangible and geographically limited, DPGs transcend physical boundaries and can be accessed globally. They encompass a wide range of open-source software, open data, open AI models, open standards and open content that support and enhance the development of digital societies. They are designed to provide universal access to essential digital infrastructure and services, ensuring that no one is left behind in the digital age. Let's look at some examples.

Linux Operating System:

Linux is an open-source operating system that serves as the backbone for many technological infrastructures, from personal computers to global supercomputers. Its open-source nature means that anyone can use, modify and distribute the software. Linux's role in powering servers, smartphones (via Android) and various embedded systems highlights its importance as a DPG that facilitates innovation and technological advancement across industries.

Wikipedia:

Wikipedia is a free online encyclopaedia that anyone can access and contribute to. It exemplifies the principles of digital public goods through its open-access model and collaborative content creation. With millions of articles in numerous languages, Wikipedia provides a vast repository of knowledge that is freely available to anyone with internet access. This democratization of information supports education and research worldwide.

OpenStreetMap:

OpenStreetMap (OSM) is a collaborative mapping project that provides free geographic data to anyone who needs it. Users can contribute to and utilize OSM data for various purposes, such as navigation, urban planning and disaster response. For example, during natural disasters, humanitarian organizations use OSM data to coordinate relief efforts and map affected areas, demonstrating its critical role in supporting global humanitarian initiatives.

Indian Examples of DPG

India has been at the forefront of developing and leveraging DPGs to promote digital inclusion, enhance public service delivery and foster economic growth. These initiatives have created a robust digital infrastructure that benefits millions of citizens. India's development and implementation of DPGs have significantly contributed to digital inclusion and the overall growth of the digital economy. Initiatives like Aadhaar, UPI, DigiLocker, BHIM and Government e Marketplace (GeM) have transformed public service delivery, financial inclusion and administrative efficiency, showcasing the potential of DPGs in fostering a more equitable and inclusive society.

1. Aadhaar
    Aadhaar is a biometric-based digital identity system that provides each Indian resident with a unique twelve-digit identification number. It is the world's largest biometric ID system and serves as a foundational digital public good in India.

    Key Features:
    *   Universal Coverage: Over 1.2 billion residents enrolled.
    *   Biometric Authentication: Uses fingerprints and iris scans for secure authentication.
    *   Integration: Widely used for various services, including banking, welfare distribution and mobile connections.

Impact:

- Direct Benefit Transfers: Ensures that subsidies and welfare benefits reach the intended beneficiaries directly, reducing leakage and corruption.
- Financial Inclusion: Facilitates the opening of bank accounts and ensures access to financial services for underserved populations.

2. UPI

   UPI is a real-time payment system that allows users to link multiple bank accounts to a single mobile application, enabling seamless and instant money transfers.

   Key Features:

   - Interoperability: Works across different banks and financial institutions.
   - Ease of Use: Simple and secure transactions using a mobile phone.
   - Scalability: Supports millions of transactions per day.

   Impact:

   - Digital Payments Revolution: Transformed the payments landscape in India, making digital transactions ubiquitous.
   - Economic Growth: Facilitated the growth of digital commerce and small businesses by providing a reliable payment method.

3. DigiLocker

   DigiLocker is a cloud-based platform for the issuance and verification of documents and certificates, enabling citizens to store and share their documents electronically.

   Key Features:

   - Secure Storage: Provides a secure and private digital space for important documents.

- Convenience: Eliminates the need for physical documents and simplifies access.
- Integration: Linked with various government departments for easy retrieval of documents.

Impact:

- Efficiency: Reduces administrative overhead and paperwork for both citizens and government agencies.
- Accessibility: Ensures that important documents are accessible anytime, anywhere.

4. GeM

GeM is an online platform for public procurement in India, facilitating the purchase of goods and services by government departments and agencies.

Key Features:

- Transparency: Ensures a transparent and efficient procurement process.
- Ease of Access: Simplifies the procurement process with a user-friendly interface.
- Wide Range: Offers a wide range of products and services from verified sellers.

Impact:

- Cost Savings: Reduces costs through competitive bidding and bulk purchasing.
- Efficiency: Streamlines the procurement process, reducing delays and administrative burdens.

Key Characteristics of DPGs

Universality:

DPGs are designed to be accessible to everyone, regardless of their location, economic status or other barriers. This universality ensures that all individuals have the opportunity to benefit from essential digital infrastructure and services. For example, the Linux operating system is available to anyone who wishes to use it, providing a robust and secure foundation for countless technological applications worldwide.

Non-excludability:

Non-excludability means that no one can be prevented from using digital public goods. Once these goods are made available, they are open to everyone. This characteristic is crucial in promoting inclusivity and equality. For instance, Wikipedia allows anyone with internet access to read and contribute to its articles, making vast amounts of knowledge freely available to all.

Non-rivalry:

Non-rivalry indicates that one person's use of a digital public good does not reduce its availability to others. This is a fundamental advantage of digital goods over physical goods. For example, when one person uses OpenStreetMap to access geographic data, it does not diminish the quality or availability of that data for others. This characteristic supports the scalability and sustainability of digital public goods.

Benefits

Democratization of Technology:

By providing free and open access to critical digital tools and resources, DPGs level the playing field, allowing individuals and organizations from all backgrounds to participate in the digital economy. For instance, the availability of open-source software like Linux enables small businesses and start-ups to build and scale their operations without the financial burden of expensive proprietary software licenses.

Innovation and Collaboration:

Open access to DPGs encourages innovation by allowing developers to build on existing tools and data. This collaborative ecosystem accelerates technological advancement and fosters a culture of continuous improvement. For example, the development of various Linux distributions, such as Ubuntu and Red Hat, illustrates how open-source software can be customized and enhanced to meet diverse user needs.

Case Study: The COVID-19 Response through DPGs

During the COVID-19 pandemic, DPGs played a vital role in the global response. Platforms like the COVID-19 Data Repository by Johns Hopkins University provided open access to crucial data, enabling researchers, policymakers and the public to track the spread of the virus and make informed decisions. Additionally, the open-source contact tracing apps developed in various countries helped control the spread of the virus by alerting individuals of potential exposure. In India, the Arogya Setu App and COVID Vaccine Intelligence Network (CoWIN) app played a major role in handling the pandemic effectively given the challenges of the large population, spread across a geographically dispersed nation.

Both Aarogya Setu and CoWIN exemplify the effective use of Digital Public Goods and Infrastructure to manage public health challenges. Aarogya Setu's role in contact tracing and information dissemination, coupled with CoWIN's efficient management of the vaccination process, highlights the transformative potential of digital tools in combating the COVID-19 pandemic. These platforms not only helped mitigate the spread of the virus but also ensured a structured and transparent vaccination campaign, showcasing the impact of digital innovation in public health management. Let us look at these two apps in detail.

Aarogya Setu App

Aarogya Setu is a mobile application developed by the National Informatics Centre under the Ministry of Electronics and Information Technology in India. It was launched on 2 April 2020, with the primary aim of tracking COVID-19 infections and facilitating contact tracing to control the spread of the virus.

Functionality:

- Contact Tracing: Aarogya Setu uses Bluetooth and GPS to track the interaction between users. When two users come in close proximity, the app records this interaction. If any user later tests positive for COVID-19, the app alerts all users who came into contact with the infected person, advising them on the next steps such as self-isolation or testing.
- Self-assessment: The app includes a self-assessment tool where users can input their health status and symptoms. Based on the input, the app provides advice on whether the user should seek medical assistance.
- Information Dissemination: Aarogya Setu provides users with the latest information and advisories from the Ministry of Health and Family Welfare. This includes updates on COVID-19 statistics, guidelines and protocols.
- E-Pass Integration: For essential workers, the app integrates an E-pass feature to facilitate movement during the lockdown.

Impact and Usage:

- Adoption: Within a few months of its launch, Aarogya Setu was downloaded over 100 million times, making it one of the fastest growing mobile applications globally. As of July 2020, it had crossed 127 million downloads.
- Identification of Hotspots: The data collected through Aarogya Setu was used to identify COVID-19 hotspots, enabling targeted interventions and resource allocation.
- Enhanced Awareness: By providing real-time information and self-assessment tools, the app helped in raising awareness and promoting preventive measures among the population.

Usage Statistics:

- Download Milestones: The app reached fifty million downloads in the first thirteen days, 100 million in forty-one days, and continued to grow rapidly. [1]
- Active Users: At its peak, Aarogya Setu had over 150 million registered users actively using the app to track their exposure and stay informed.

CoWIN App

CoWIN is a digital platform developed to manage the vaccination process across India. It was introduced in January 2021 to streamline the registration, scheduling and certification of COVID-19 vaccinations.

Functionality:

- Registration and Scheduling: Individuals can register for vaccination through the CoWIN portal or mobile app,

---

[1] 'Aarogya Setu', *Wikipedia*, November 13, 2024, https://en.wikipedia.org/wiki/Aarogya_Setu

select their preferred vaccination centre and schedule appointments. The platform supports multiple languages to cater to diverse user groups.

- Real-time Monitoring: CoWIN provides real-time monitoring of vaccine distribution and administration, ensuring transparency and efficiency. It tracks vaccine stocks, cold chain management and beneficiary coverage.
- Certification: After receiving the vaccine, individuals can download their vaccination certificates directly from the CoWIN platform. This certificate includes a QR code for verification.
- Integration with Aarogya Setu: CoWIN is integrated with the Aarogya Setu app to provide a seamless user experience and ensure easy access to vaccination information.

Impact and Usage:

- Vaccination Drive: CoWIN played a critical role in managing one of the world's largest vaccination drives. It facilitated the administration of millions of vaccine doses daily, ensuring orderly and efficient vaccine distribution.
- Transparency and Accountability: The real-time data provided by CoWIN allowed for transparency and accountability in the vaccination process. Authorities could track vaccine usage, manage supplies and prevent wastage effectively.
- Ease of Access: By allowing individuals to register, schedule and obtain vaccination certificates online, CoWIN made the vaccination process more accessible and convenient for the public.

Usage Statistics:

- Vaccine Doses Administered: By July 2021, CoWIN had facilitated the administration of over 400 million vaccine doses. As of January 2022, the platform recorded over 1.5 billion vaccine doses administered.

- User Registration: Millions of users registered on CoWIN to schedule their vaccinations, reflecting the platform's wide reach and adoption.
- Global Recognition: The success of CoWIN's implementation has drawn interest from other countries looking to develop similar systems for their vaccination programmes.

Educational Impact:

DPGs have a significant impact on education by providing students and educators with free access to a wealth of resources. Platforms like Khan Academy, that offers free online courses and educational materials, empower learners worldwide to access high-quality education regardless of their socio-economic backgrounds. This accessibility supports lifelong learning and helps bridge educational gaps.

Digital Public Infrastructure and India Stack

Just as physical roads connect people and facilitate the movement of goods and services, DPI connects individuals and enables the flow of digital services. It forms the backbone of a digital economy, allowing people to access essential services like banking, healthcare and education with ease.

DPI refers to the foundational digital systems and platforms that enable the delivery of essential services to the public. These systems are designed to be open, interoperable and inclusive, ensuring that they can be used by a wide range of stakeholders, including governments, businesses and individuals. DPI includes components such as digital identification systems, payment infrastructures and data exchange solutions. The primary goal of DPI is to facilitate the efficient flow of people, money and information, thereby empowering citizens and improving their quality of life. Several new start-ups and businesses have been built on top of such Digital Public Infrastructure and India Stack as it is commonly known. We will delve into the evolution and how government initiatives helped spur the new business models.

India Stack is a comprehensive set of open APIs and digital public goods that collectively form the backbone of India's digital public infrastructure. It aims to unlock the economic imperatives of identity, data and payments at a population scale. India Stack is designed to provide a secure, interoperable and scalable platform for the delivery of various services, promoting financial and social inclusion.

To better understand India Stack, think of it as a digital infrastructure that provides essential tools for building modern services, much like how physical infrastructure supports transportation and commerce. India Stack comprises several layers that work together to deliver a wide range of services securely and efficiently.

Four Layers of India Stack:

1. Presenceless Layer:
   - Aadhaar Authentication: This layer enables users to authenticate their identity digitally using Aadhaar, eliminating the need for physical presence.

   Aadhaar is the world's largest biometric identification system, which provides a unique digital identity to over a billion Indian citizens. This digital ID can be used for various purposes, such as opening a bank account or receiving government subsidies, ensuring that even the most underserved populations have access to essential financial services.

2. Paperless Layer:
   - DigiLocker and e-Sign: These tools facilitate the digital storage and sharing of documents and the use of electronic signatures.

   DigiLocker provides a secure cloud-based platform where individuals can store and share important documents, such as driver's licenses and academic certificates. This eliminates the need for carrying physical copies and enables the easy verification of documents for various services, like applying for jobs or enrolling in educational programs. [2]

3. Cashless Layer:
   - UPI: This system allows instant money transfers between bank accounts through mobile phones.

   With UPI, even a small vendor or street seller can accept digital payments seamlessly, promoting financial inclusion and reducing the dependency on cash. For instance, someone buying vegetables from a local market can pay directly using a simple QR code, making transactions quick and easy for both the customer and the seller.

   UPI has revolutionized digital payments in India, with applications like Google Pay, PhonePe and Paytm facilitating billions of transactions on a monthly basis.

4. Consent Layer:
   - Digital Consent Management: Provides a secure and user-friendly way to manage consent for data sharing.
   - The Account Aggregator framework enables users to share their financial data with third parties (like banks or financial advisors) securely and with full consent.

   Consider the **Account Aggregator framework**, which is part of the Consent Layer. Suppose a person wants to apply

---

[2] 'DigiLocker', *DigiLocker*, November 13, 2024, https://www.digilocker.gov.in/

for a loan. Instead of physically submitting bank statements and other financial documents to the lender, they can use an Account Aggregator to grant digital consent. This allows the lender to access the necessary financial data directly from the person's bank, but only for the purpose of evaluating the loan application. The user has full visibility into what data is being shared, with whom and for how long. Once the purpose is fulfilled, the consent can be withdrawn, and the data access is terminated.

Transformation and Impact through Strong Digital Public Infrastructure

The development of India Stack has created a seamless, scalable and secure digital infrastructure, underpinning various digital services and applications across the country. It has created nationwide impact and also helped new business models to emerge.

- Financial Inclusion: The UPI system has brought millions of unbanked and underbanked individuals into the formal financial system. For instance, small vendors and shopkeepers can now accept digital payments, reducing reliance on cash.
- Streamlined Services: Services like Aadhaar and DigiLocker have significantly reduced paperwork and processing times for various government and private sector services. For example, DigiLocker integration in the transport sector allows traffic police to verify documents without needing physical copies.

- India Stack has enabled the emergence of innovative business models, particularly in fintech, health tech and EdTech sectors, by providing a robust digital backbone.
- Fintech Innovation: Companies like BharatPe, which provides digital payment solutions to small merchants, and Zerodha, a discount brokerage firm leveraging Aadhaar-based KYC for quick account opening, exemplify fintech innovations driven by India Stack.

Healthcare providers use Aadhaar authentication for patient verification and DigiLocker for storing and sharing medical records, improving healthcare delivery and patient management.

These initiatives have not only transformed public service delivery but also spurred innovation across various sectors, fostering a more inclusive and efficient digital economy.

ONDC: Revolutionizing Digital Commerce in India

ONDC represents a groundbreaking initiative aimed at democratizing the digital commerce landscape in India. Launched by the Government of India, ONDC seeks to create an open, interoperable and decentralized network that enables SMEs, local businesses and start-ups to compete with large e-commerce giants.

ONDC simplifies access to e-commerce infrastructure and data for start-ups and tech entrepreneurs, enabling them to develop innovative solutions and enter the expansive e-commerce market with ease.

ONDC - Open Network for Digital Commerce

- <u>Decentralised</u>
- Unbundled
- Open and Interoperable Network as against a platform
- Population scale infrastructure to enable e-commerce

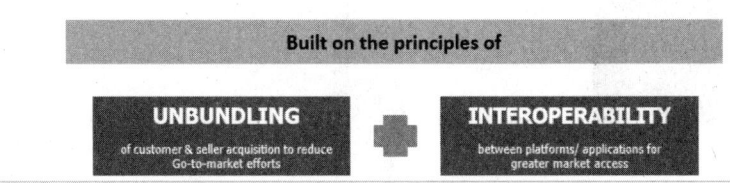

Source: ONDC strategy paper

ONDC functions as an intermediary in the online shopping ecosystem, facilitating connections between buyers and sellers. Users can access ONDC through various channels called Bueyr apps, such as the Paytm app or the official ONDC website. For example, within the food section, users can order from both small, local businesses and well-known food chains. This integration of different providers offers consumers more choices and competitive prices, fostering healthy competition. The same principle applies to other categories, including groceries, home decor, electronics and more. ONDC empowers consumers to select items from a broad spectrum of vendors, ranging from small neighbourhood stores to large supermarket chains, providing the freedom to explore various products and find the best deals.

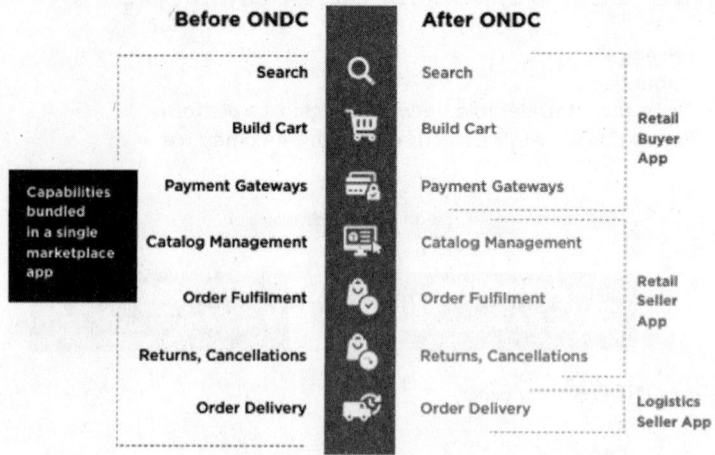

ONDC **unbundles** the e-commerce components and leverages open protocols so that
the unbundled components are **interoperable** in the network.

Structure and Functioning of ONDC

Core Components:

ONDC operates on a set of core principles and components designed to facilitate an open and inclusive digital commerce ecosystem:

- Open Protocols: ONDC is built on open protocols that enable interoperability among different e-commerce platforms. This ensures that sellers and buyers on one platform can seamlessly interact with those on another.
- Decentralized Network: Unlike traditional e-commerce models, ONDC is a decentralized network where no single entity has control. This decentralization fosters competition and innovation.

- Standardization: The network promotes standardization in terms of product listings, payment mechanisms and delivery processes, making it easier for businesses to participate.

Technology and Innovation:

ONDC leverages cutting-edge technologies such as blockchain, AI and ML to ensure secure, efficient and transparent transactions. Blockchain technology, for instance, is used to create a tamper-proof ledger of transactions, enhancing trust and security. AI and ML are employed to personalize user experiences, optimize supply chain operations and provide actionable insights to businesses.

Benefits of ONDC

For Small and Medium Enterprises:

- Increased Market Access: ONDC provides SMEs with access to a larger customer base, enabling them to expand their reach and grow their businesses.
- Lower Costs: By reducing reliance on intermediaries and large e-commerce platforms, ONDC helps SMEs to lower their operational costs.
- Enhanced Competitiveness: The standardized and interoperable nature of ONDC levels the playing field, allowing SMEs to compete with larger players on an equal footing.

For Consumers:

- Greater Choice: ONDC offers consumers a wider range of products and services by aggregating offerings from multiple sellers.

- Competitive Pricing: The presence of multiple sellers on a single platform fosters competition, leading to better prices for consumers.
- Improved Trust: The use of advanced technologies such as blockchain ensures secure and transparent transactions, enhancing consumer trust.

For the Economy:

- Digital Inclusion: ONDC promotes digital inclusion by enabling more businesses to participate in the digital economy, driving economic growth.
- Job Creation: The expansion of digital commerce creates new job opportunities in sectors such as logistics, technology and customer service.
- Innovation and Entrepreneurship: ONDC fosters innovation by providing a platform for start-ups and entrepreneurs to launch and scale their businesses.

Case Studies and Examples of ONDC Applications

ONDC has enabled local artisans in rural India to access a broader market for their handcrafted products. By listing their products on the network, artisans can reach customers across the country, bypassing traditional supply chain limitations. This has led to increased sales, higher incomes and greater recognition of their craftsmanship.

Farmers and agricultural cooperatives have benefited from ONDC by directly connecting with buyers and eliminating middlemen. This direct access to the market ensures better prices for their produce and reduces the time taken to sell their products.

For instance, a farmer in Maharashtra can now sell fresh produce to consumers in Mumbai, ensuring freshness and higher returns.

1. PhonePe's Pincode App:
   - PhonePe launched a new shopping app called Pincode, built on the ONDC platform. The app focuses on hyperlocal commerce, connecting local buyers and sellers and benefiting other ecosystem participants like last-mile logistics and inventory management players.
2. Woolly Farms:
   - During the pilot phase, Bengaluru-based Woolly Farms received the first ONDC order from the Paytm app, marking the first transaction on the network. This example highlights the potential of ONDC to facilitate seamless transactions and support local businesses.
3. 'ONDC Startup Mahotsav':
   The 'ONDC Startup Mahotsav' is a unique collaboration between ONDC and the Startup India initiative. The event benefited from the participation of over 150 start-ups and twelve unicorns, including EaseMyTrip, Of Business and Zerodha. More than five lakh sellers have been onboarded on the platform, of which more than 70 per cent are small or medium-sized sellers. In April 2024, ONDC facilitated around 7.22 million transactions.

Impact of ONDC

1. Economic Growth and Inclusion:
   - By democratizing access to digital commerce, ONDC is expected to drive economic growth and foster inclusion. It provides opportunities for small businesses to compete with larger players, promoting entrepreneurship and economic development.

2. Enhanced Supply Chain Efficiency:
    *   ONDC's emphasis on standardized processes and technologies can significantly streamline supply chain operations, reducing costs and improving delivery times. This benefits both businesses and consumers.
3. Increased Competition and Reduced Costs:
    *   The open network model promotes healthy competition, leading to reduced costs for businesses and consumers. Increased competition among e-commerce service providers drives down transaction fees, commissions and advertising costs.
4. Rural Empowerment:
    *   By extending e-commerce accessibility to rural areas, ONDC empowers rural consumers and businesses, opening up new markets and opportunities. This outreach is crucial for bridging the digital divide and promoting inclusive growth.
5. Innovation and Start-up Ecosystem:
    *   ONDC fosters a vibrant start-up ecosystem by providing a platform for innovation and collaboration. Start-ups can leverage the open network to develop new products and services, driving technological advancements and economic growth.

Case Study—Namma Yatri: Leveraging DPI to Revolutionize Urban Transportation

In the bustling city of Bengaluru, a new wave of innovation in urban transportation is taking root through the Namma Yatri platform. Namma Yatri, which translates to 'Our Journey,' is a shining example of how DPI and DPG can transform traditional services into more efficient, inclusive and user-friendly solutions.

This initiative leverages the foundational principles of India Stack to create a robust, scalable and transparent model for urban mobility, significantly benefiting both riders and drivers.

As of November 2024, Namma Yatri has rapidly scaled its operations, boasting an impressive network of 5.2 lakh enabled drivers and serving a robust user base of 88 lakh regular users. The platform's commitment to driver empowerment and transparent fare distribution has translated into significant financial benefits, with total driver earnings reaching an extraordinary Rs1000 crore. This impressive scale is further highlighted by the successful completion of 6.3 crore trips, reflecting the platform's ability to meet high demand while maintaining efficiency and user satisfaction.

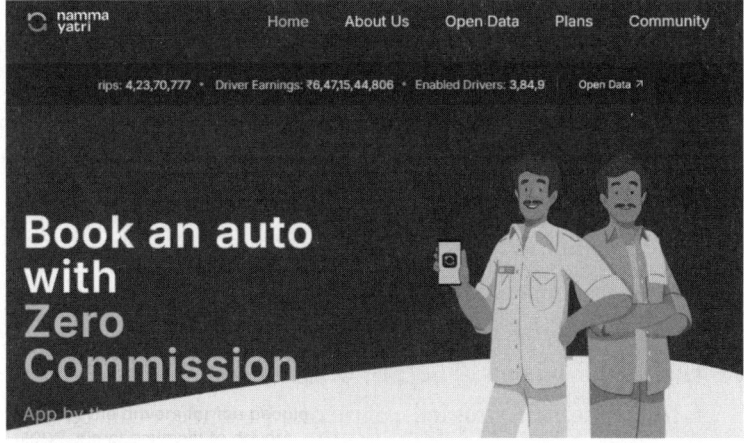

Customer-friendly, Namma Yatri is a mobility application built with a vision of effectively contributing to the Open Mobility initiative. The application has been built on the Beckn Protocol which is an open-source protocol.

Unlike conventional ride-hailing services that charge high commissions, Namma Yatri operates on a minimal commission structure, ensuring that a larger share of earnings goes directly to the drivers.

By leveraging existing DPI and focusing on a lean operational model, Namma Yatri can scale its services without significant increases in overhead costs. The app passes on the entire fare paid by the customer to the driver, unlike Uber or Ola or other platforms that retain a substantial commission. The platform's focus on fair pricing and driver empowerment fosters community support and loyalty, aiding in organic growth and user retention.

Key Features:

1. Digital Ride-hailing: Passengers can book autorickshaws through a user-friendly mobile app. The app allows users to enter their destination, view available drivers nearby and select a ride.

2. Real-time Tracking: Once a ride is booked, passengers can track the location of their autorickshaw in real time, receive updates on estimated time of arrival (ETA) and communicate with the driver, if necessary.

3. Transparent Pricing: Namma Yatri uses a standardized fare system, which is calculated based on distance and time. This eliminates the need for fare negotiations and ensures fairness for both passengers and drivers.

4. Cashless Payments: The platform integrates with UPI to facilitate seamless digital payments. Passengers can pay for their rides directly through the app, ensuring secure and quick transactions.

5. Driver Verification: The service includes a stringent verification process for drivers, using Aadhaar-based digital identity checks to ensure the safety and reliability of the drivers on the platform.

6. Secure Document Storage: Drivers and passengers can use DigiLocker to store and share essential documents

electronically, reducing the need for physical copies and enhancing convenience.

Namma Yatri exemplifies how digital public infrastructure and goods can transform urban transportation. Its innovative service model and sustainable business practices provide a blueprint for integrating traditional services into the digital economy, offering enhanced benefits for drivers, passengers and the broader community.

Key Takeaways

- Empowerment through Digital Technology:
  o DPGs and DPI democratize access to technology and services, enabling small businesses and individuals to reach larger markets and improve their economic prospects.
- Examples of DPGs:
  o Linux Operating System: An open-source software powering diverse technological infrastructures.
  o Wikipedia: A free, collaboratively created encyclopaedia.
  o OpenStreetMap: A global, user-contributed mapping project.
  o Indian Initiatives: Aadhaar, UPI, DigiLocker and GeM, which enhance public service delivery and economic growth.
- Key Characteristics of DPGs:
  o Universality: Accessible to everyone regardless of location or economic status.
  o Non-Excludability: Open to all users without exclusion.
  o Non-Rivalry: One person's use does not make it less available to others.
- Benefits of Digital Public Goods:
  o Democratization of Technology: Levels the playing field for all participants in the digital economy.

- o Innovation and Collaboration: Encourages development and enhancement of existing tools and data.
- Impact of COVID-19:
  - o DPGs played a critical role in managing the pandemic through data sharing, contact tracing and vaccination management (Aarogya Setu and CoWIN apps in India).
- India Stack and Digital Public Infrastructure:
  - o Presenceless Layer: Aadhaar for digital identity verification.
  - o Paperless Layer: DigiLocker and e-Sign for digital document management.
  - o Cashless Layer: UPI for real-time payments.
  - o Consent Layer: Digital consent management for secure data sharing.
- Transformation through DPI:
  - o Financial Inclusion: UPI has brought millions into the formal financial system.
  - o Streamlined Services: Aadhaar and DigiLocker reduce paperwork and expedite service delivery.
- ONDC:
  - o Aims to democratize e-commerce, enabling SMEs and local businesses to compete with larger e-commerce platforms.
  - o Utilizes open protocols and decentralized networks for interoperability and standardization.
  - o Benefits include increased market access for SMEs, reduced costs and greater choice for consumers.
- Case Studies and Applications:
  - o PhonePe's Pincode App: Facilitates hyperlocal commerce.
  - o Woolly Farms: An example of seamless transactions through ONDC.
  - o Namma Yatri: Uses DPI to revolutionize urban transportation in Bengaluru.

- Economic and Social Impact:
  - o Economic Growth and Inclusion: ONDC drives economic development and fosters inclusion.
  - o Rural Empowerment: Extends e-commerce access to rural areas, bridging the digital divide.
  - o Innovation and Entrepreneurship: Encourages start-ups to leverage open networks for business growth.

10

Digital Transformation of Legacy Businesses Leveraging New Business Models

Over the last few decades, businesses have been challenged to reimagine themselves in the age of digital technologies. Who would have thought that, across demographics and geographies, customers would use their mobile phones to buy, learn and manage their finances and health with so much ease? COVID-19 further accelerated the need for the digital transformation of various sectors. Suddenly, the only way in which people could access healthcare was through tele-consultation and by getting medicines delivered at home. This meant that even the most conventional of hospitals and doctors had to incorporate digital methods of attending to their patients. While COVID-19 was an accelerator, this transition has been going on for the past decade or more, with various sectors showing different levels of acceptance.

This chapter discusses how existing traditional businesses can thrive and compete with new disruptive companies in their space. We discuss how to use digital transformation as a competitive tool and redesign the business model, leveraging the Internet, data and techology.

Digital Transformation of Business: Common Terminologies

The terms digitization, digitalization and digital transformation are often used interchangeably, but they actually refer to different stages of integrating digital technology into business processes. Here's a clear explanation of each, along with examples:

Digitization is the process of converting analogue or physical information into a digital format. This is the first step in any digital initiative, where the main goal is to transform existing paper-based or manual processes into digital ones.

For example, converting paper records into digital files by scanning documents or using software to digitize financial records. A hospital, for instance, might scan patient paper records and store them electronically, making them easier to access and manage.

Digitalization goes a step further by using digital data to improve or automate existing business processes. The focus here is on enhancing efficiency and improving the experience by leveraging digital tools, but without fundamentally changing the way a business operates.

For example, a Human Resource department moving from a manual, paper-based employee onboarding process to a digital platform that allows new hires to complete forms online, sign documents electronically and receive automated email updates.

Digital transformation is a more profound shift that fundamentally changes how a business operates and delivers value to its customers. It involves rethinking business models, culture and strategies to fully leverage digital technology. Digital transformation is about using digital technology to create new or improved ways of working, engaging with customers and generating revenue.

For example, Netflix's evolution from a DVD rental service to a global streaming platform is a classic example of digital transformation. By leveraging digital technology, Netflix not only digitized its DVD rental service but also transformed its business model to deliver on-demand streaming and personalized content recommendations. Another example is a traditional retailer shifting from purely brick-and-mortar operations to an omnichannel model, using data analytics and AI to personalize the customer shopping experience both online and in-store.

Each of these stages builds on the previous one, with digital transformation being the most comprehensive and impactful change.

Banking Industry Context—From Digitization to Digitalization to Digital Transformation

1. Digitization in Banking
   - Banks converting paper records and forms into digital formats.
     - o Traditionally, banks kept customer information and transaction records in paper files. With digitization, they scan these documents and store them in secure digital databases. This makes data easier to retrieve and reduces the need for physical storage space.

    o This step only converts information into digital form but doesn't change the way banks operate.

2. Digitalization in Banking
   - Automating routine banking processes.
     - o After digitizing records, banks start using digital platforms to streamline operations. For instance, instead of having customers fill out forms in person at a branch, banks offer online applications for account opening, loan approvals and fund transfers. Mobile banking apps allow customers to check their balances, pay bills and manage transactions from their phones.
     - o Banking processes become more efficient and convenient, but the core business model (i.e., providing financial services) remains largely the same. The bank uses technology to enhance existing services rather than completely transforming how it operates.

3. Digital Transformation in Banking
   - Reimagining banking through new digital business models.
     - o A bank goes beyond just automating services to fundamentally changing how it operates. For example, a traditional bank might develop a digital-only bank that has no physical branches. This new digital bank could use advanced analytics to provide personalized financial advice, AI-driven chatbots for customer service, and blockchain for secure and transparent transactions. Additionally, it might offer features like fully automated loan approvals using AI, or real-time insights into spending habits to help customers manage their finances better.

Now is the time for such a transformation.

The last decade has seen significant changes in technology which gives businesses an opportunity to reimagine their offerings and approach towards the market. From cloud computing and data analytics to IoT and AI, there have been numerous and continuous developments in the space in a short while.

Customer expectations have gone up dramatically. With a huge uptake of smartphones across the world, and even more so in India, customers have come to expect the ease of digital access in all sectors. What started in gaming/shopping and such sectors has moved to other core sectors such as healthcare and education. Large businesses in the core sectors including telecom, banking and insurance, have had to transform themselves to meet these changing expectations.

A new competitive landscape has emerged with digital-first or digital-only players in many of the traditional sectors. These offer new solutions to customers, in a manner that is frictionless, while also working with significantly lower cost of operations and overheads. For example, fintechs have been offering low-cost banking, payments and credit solutions to customers and have started to be serious competitors to the traditional banking sector.

Manufacturing, too, is undergoing transformation due to IoT, robotics, AI, ML and information technology, referred to as Industry 4.0.

Key Dimensions of Digital Transformation

The adoption of technologies helps in multiple dimensions—internal dimensions of products and processes and externally from the perspective of customer experience.

Creating new products/offerings that would not have been possible earlier: Banks, with the help of digital technologies, have started offering complete end-to-end digital journeys for their customers. This implies that the customers need not ever visit a branch, be it for opening accounts, or for conducting transactions of any nature. This can attract a whole new generation of customers who are familiar and prefer digital modes of working. Today, with many of the private banks, you can download their apps and open a new digital account with the help of a virtual KYC process. These customers can then operate their account digitally for savings, loan, investments, etc. Earlier, banks could only cater to customers in the neighbourhood of their branches. Today there is no restriction on geography to get new customers. Online payments using UPI is another example of a whole new digital product which did not exist a few years ago. Today, through Google Pay, PhonePe or Paytm, using UPI capabilities, we can make payments across a very large number of establishments and shops, big and small. A huge number of customers are now transacting without tendering cash for transactions in the retail space. This is expected to grow to a billion transactions per day in the next couple of years.

Reimagining processes: Technologies can help in improving the efficiency of processes. They can even completely reimagine how work gets done. One such example is seen in the area of supply chain management. Using IoT, sensors in the warehouses, transportation vehicles and in factories, it is possible to automate the management of inventory levels. By connecting this system to the material suppliers, automation of refill and creation of just-in-time inventory can be made possible. This can help not just in ensuring zero stock-outs but can also optimize the inventory carrying costs.

Reimagining customer experience: The use of the digital journeys of customers can help in capturing data about their preferences, buying behaviours and expectations relating to their experience. This can help in crafting experiences that are customized and relevant to customers, reducing friction and improving customer revenues. Examples of this range from the presentation of appropriate assortments, suggestions of additional products to buy, virtual trials, speedy delivery, etc. Quick commerce/Qcommerce has emerged as a new category, with companies such as Zepto, Blinkit and now even BigBasket promising to deliver groceries within ten minutes of ordering. It is quite extraordinary to imagine that while cooking, you suddenly realize that you need an ingredient that you are missing. You whip out your phone, order it and within ten minutes, you receive it and continue with your cooking without having to make an urgent trip to the market!

Framework for Digital Transformation of Business:

True digital transformation of an organization is like changing the wheels of an airplane while it is flying. It requires careful planning and execution. It is essential to have measures to review the progress and keep aligning efforts towards the objectives that are set up early on. Having the organization fully aligned towards this transformation is essential and requires strong change management with executive sponsorship and operational support. Understanding the current business model:

This step of understanding the existing model serves as the foundation for the rest of the journey of digital transformation. The existing model defines how your company delivers value to its customers, generates revenues and delivers economic value to stakeholders. It is the confluence of the target audience, the customer journeys, processes and technology frameworks that are currently operational. While it may be exciting to look at the latest trends in technology and evaluate/roll out in specific aspects of your operations, it would be better to carry out a baseline assessment of the current state of your business, the ecosystem that it operates in and then put together a plan for the future.

Some of the key tools that could be used for this purpose include:

Business model canvas: This is a strategic management template, developed initially by Alexander Osterwalder, that helps in documenting an existing business using a visual chart with nine building blocks: customer segments, value propositions, channels, customer relationships, revenue streams, key resources, key activities, key partnerships and cost structure.[1]

SWOT analysis of the business: Studying the strengths and weaknesses from the inside out, while looking at opportunities and threats from the outside in can help us assess the current status correctly.

Customer feedback: Customers can provide the best feedback on the quality of products and services that they receive from the company. A comparison with competitive alternatives and new features and capabilities would be of interest to them. DBS went through its first round of transformation in 2009, the core driver of which was to improve customer service standards substantially, with a view to becoming the Asian Bank of Choice.

Employee feedback: Employees, especially those on the frontline who interact with customers on a regular basis, can be extremely valuable in providing insights on where the challenges and opportunities lie for the business. They can share

---

[1] Source: www.alexosterwalder.com

information on the changing expectations of customers, and on new entrants into the market who might disrupt the business in the near future.

Market analysis: Study your metrics as compared to those of your competitors, both traditional and new, who might come from different industries or contexts. The second wave of digital transformation in DBS was triggered by the wave of fintechs that were emerging from China and impacting the Asian market for financial services.

Identifying Opportunities for Transformation: A study of the existing business model, a comparison with the market and feedback from customers and employees can help you identify the gaps and opportunities that you can explore. This can further help identify the core theme that will form the foundation of the transformation plan.

These themes could arise out of the following:

Customer-centric opportunities: Access to digital technologies is changing the expectations that customers have from businesses. They expect an always-on experience, high-quality and diverse product assortments, quick turnarounds, and seamless interactions. Interestingly, while this expectation has been more pronounced in the B2C offerings, it has also started to impact the expectations of the B2B clientele. In the banking industry, digital journeys started with B2C customers. However, now most private banks in India have built very comprehensive digital journeys for their corporate clients. This has been driven by the demands of B2B clients who want the same experience that they get as individual users, with the maturity and controls that their environment demands.

One way to do this would be to identify the key drivers for customer-centric digital transformation. The objectives could include improving CLTV, by improving the customer experience, predicting customer needs and fulfilling them proactively. For instance, in the e-commerce industry, creating a frictionless experience is important. This means that it should be very easy for the customer to discover the products that they wish to buy and the process of order completion; the payment should be smooth too. The delivery needs to be seamless, with all the items asked for being delivered. The last step is for the returns and refunds process to be predictable and reassuring. Amazon has perfected this experience to the extent that the need to talk to a human to solve any customer service problems is minimized. Many e-commerce companies, from Amazon to Flipkart, have used the customer experience as their North Star for their digital objectives. A combination of good customer experience and a wide assortment of product choices can increase the frequency of purchase and lead to significant improvement in the lifetime revenue of customers, thus leading to improved economics.

In 2015, when DBS rolled out its 'Making banking joyful' vision, they embarked on an objective to make banking invisible. They wanted to ensure that as customers went about their day-to-day work, be it managing monthly expenses or buying a new house, the bank played a crucial role without adding any friction to the transaction.[2]

Operational Efficiencies and Cost Effectiveness

This is a very important dimension for considering the introduction of technology into any organization, including those in the manufacturing sector. A combination of computing

---

[2] How we create value – our business model | DBS Annual Report 2017; How DBS Became the 'World's Best Bank' | INSEAD Knowledge

power, data analytics, IoT, robotics and other automation technologies has helped improve supply chain economics, cost and quality of manufacturing, and the agility of manufacturing multiple products on the same lines. One example is that of a leading consumer packaged goods company which has deployed end-to-end digital solutions to improve their supply chain efficiency. They have connected the systems used by the local retailers/kirana store, to their distributors, which in turn are connected to their systems. They get real-time information of the inventories and velocity of sales across the entire network and use this to optimize their production and despatch plans. This has helped reduce the inventory of finished goods across their network, while minimizing stock-outs at retail outlets.

L&T has a very large and distributed construction business, spread over 400 sites at any time. While they had deployed IT for managing their business processes, i.e., ERP, finance, etc., they realized that their core business was not benefiting from digital technology. They had a very large number of machines and equipment, 35,000 in number, deployed across their sites and they realized that using digital technology to manage the utilization of these sites could be a game changer for them. They connected this equipment using IoT sensors and started publishing utilization data. Over a period of time, they saw significant improvement in the utilization of equipment, better process management and more thoughtful equipment purchase.

Products and Services Innovation

Many sectors have seen big changes on deploying digital technology to create new products and services. The healthcare sector, with a combination of mobile technology at the patient end, digitalization of patient records, AI and ML, have been able to bring in a whole host of remote healthcare solutions. These solutions range from tele-consultation to remote diagnosis and personalized medicine. None of these offerings would have been possible without using technology across the different parts of the healthcare system. In the area of cancer care, specialized diagnostic methods that use a combination of radiology and AI are able to come up with very early diagnosis of certain types of cancers, leading to better outcomes for patients. One of the big challenges faced in cancer care in India is access to expertise in the smaller cities and towns. Most large cancer centres, which house the well-known experts, are typically located in the big cities and metros. The National Cancer Grid (NCG) has been set up to connect cancer care centres of all sizes and capabilities across the country. This allows for sharing of data, obtaining a second opinion and ensuring uniform standard of care across the country. Digital platforms for capturing patient data, case studies of cancer treatments and tele-consultation with experts have been deployed to facilitate a uniform standard of care.

New Market Expansion: Geographical and Customer Type

The banking sector has used end-to-end digital journeys to get whole new customer categories into their fold. The fintechs reached out to younger and digitally native customers, offering them credit products of various kinds. They were able to do so not just because they had access to these customers, but also because they were able to qualify them better owing to the data that they collected about them. This has forced the banks to bring in more data collection and analytics capabilities, in order to ensure the agility and speed of transactions that is expected by this customer base.

Top management institutes in India have a limitation on the number of students that they can take on campus, and getting admission can be very challenging and competitive. Using technology, many of these institutes have started offering off-campus programmes, wherein students from other locations, or even working professionals, are able to take advantage of the top management teachers' expertise and get certification from these top institutes.

Technology-Driven Opportunities:

The introduction of new technologies over the last decade has spurred many businesses to relook at their processes to take advantage of these developments. Ranging from cloud computing to IoT to ML and now generative AI, each era brought about new opportunities of transformation. Generative AI, for instance, prompted customer contact centres to completely reimagine their approach. The combination of fewer humans, supported by Gen AI tools and pilots, can transform the quality and cost of customer service meaningfully.

Netflix is an excellent case study of a company that has transformed itself multiple times with the evolution of technology over the last couple of decades. The company started in 1999 as a mail order DVD rental service. They used the technology that was available in those days, i.e., low-speed internet, and offered online ordering of DVDs, which were then delivered to homes in a few days. However, this was not competitive enough, as customers could go across to the local blockbuster and pick up DVDs that they wished to see.

As internet speeds grew and streaming technology matured, they pivoted to a movie streaming service; this turned their fortunes around. As their customer and viewing volumes grew, the data that they collected became an extremely valuable weapon, and they started providing recommendations to customers based on their viewing history. Their user interface too is one of the best, with excellent intuitive features, leading to high degree of customer loyalty. The viewing data analytics has also been instrumental in helping them identify and create original content, many of which were huge successes, e.g., *Narcos, Stranger Things, Orange Is the New Black,* etc.

Environmental Changes:

The energy sector has been undergoing substantial changes over the last decade. One change is seen in the field of energy transmission. The technology of transmission is moving to high voltage direct current; an energy 'super highway' could be one way to describe this. Another key development in the transmission space has to do with connected grids. India transitioned to a connected grid a little more than a decade ago. This meant that the monitoring of grids continuously and remotely and responding to demand–supply mismatches in real time has become critical. The impact of this on the entire energy system technology providers has been immense. They have all had to create new digital products for grid automation and monitoring, as well as offer digital services for monitoring and providing maintenance services remotely.

Siemens Energy has developed several advanced digital products for grid automation and monitoring. One of their key offerings is the *SIPROTEC* protection relays and *SICAM* automation systems, which provide real-time monitoring and automation of energy grids, ensuring efficient and seamless operations.

Schneider Electric has made significant advancements in energy automation and grid management through their

EcoStruxure Grid platform. This platform offers sophisticated monitoring, analytics and automation capabilities, empowering utilities to manage and maintain grid infrastructure remotely. Leveraging IoT and digital twin technology, Schneider Electric has enabled more efficient and reliable energy distribution.

Hitachi Energy has contributed to this digital transformation with their *Network Manager* software suite. This technology provides real-time monitoring and control of electrical grids, efficiently integrating renewable energy sources while managing supply and demand. Additionally, Hitachi Energy's digital maintenance services utilize data analytics and AI to predict and address potential grid failures proactively, ensuring the reliability and efficiency of energy transmission.

The second important transition in this sector is the energy production, transitioning to clean sources of solar and wind. This too has challenged the manufacturers and service providers to move to newer digital methods of connecting new and traditional production systems and of managing demand–supply across them.

Implementing the Transformation

Successful digital transformation would need the following three steps:

1. Starting with the most appropriate opportunity
2. Creating an enabling environment
3. Driving the change

Opportunity identification and building a roll-out plan:

Prior to designing the new business model and processes, it is important to take an inventory of the current technology deployment and state of its maturity in the organization. In the banking industry, the core platforms that run all the important business functions are very complex and, in many cases, monolithic systems. In this context, creating end-to-end digital journeys for diverse customer types can be very challenging. Building advanced and agile digital layers that work well with the existing systems, while ensuring that the compliance and regulatory needs of the banking industry are met, is a big task.

Tata Steel, under the leadership of T.V. Narendran, started a journey of transformation in 2013, when he took charge as the CEO.

Since the industry, and hence the company, was in the doldrums, his first priority was to relook at the economic viability of the company and make a strong move towards improved profitability. Digital transformation was seen as a core aspect of the business transformation that Tata Steel was embarking on. Opportunity identification for digital transformation was carried out by looking at the business 'inside out' as well as 'outside in'.

One of the opportunities selected was to use digital technology to improve the quality of products by eliminating defects during production. This was essentially a manual process of inspecting the coils/sheets at the end of the production process. This was replaced by a digital 'surface inspection system'. Sensors were installed across the entire production system. Data collected across the production journey was analysed with the help of AI and ML, to identify defects and also to determine where and why the defects were getting generated. This helped in significantly improving the quality of the product.

Creating an Enabling Environment

A change of this magnitude would require alignment across the organization and all other stakeholders that are involved/

impacted by this change. A strong and clear vision, communicated and supported by the leadership, is an essential starting point. Ensuring that this vision is shared and continuously reinforced is the foundation of getting alignment across the organization. It helps to have a clear and simple 'rallying cry', e.g., in the case of DBS, as discussed earlier, the incoming CEO, Piyush Gupta set up Vision 1.0 as 'Asia's bank of choice for the New Asia' in 2009–10.

Tata Steel hired a CIO, who had many decades of experience in the digitalization of large enterprises but also felt like a good fit into the culture of Tata Steel. The new CIO started by upgrading the core IT systems of the organization and creating a digital mindset in the leadership team. The CEO and CIO were clear that the digital transformation had to be owned and led by the business, with the technology team providing the infrastructure and skills. They created a reverse mentoring programme, putting together a team of below thirty-year-olds, tasked with upskilling the senior management, including the CEO, on digital technology and its benefits.

DBS too put in similar efforts. They set up a transformation centre, a team of about seventy people, who understood the technologies being deployed and were tasked with the role of helping the various business teams in their digitalization journey. This team possessed the toolkits that were to be used by the business teams to remodel the processes, while creating new ways of working using technologies, and they trained the business teams in these toolkits. The second key challenge was to create a 'data-driven mindset' in the organization. DBS went about training large parts of the organization on the importance of clean, good-quality data collection, analytics and decision-making using this data.

Driving the Change

The most effective way of driving change is to constantly measure and share the progress with all the relevant stakeholders. This can create a positive loop of reinforcement. The measures can also alert the organization to any deviation from plans or failures of programmes, which can then lead to course correction. In 2015, guided by its customer-oriented mission, DBS set up a balanced scorecard which gave a significant weightage to the metrics related to the customer journey and satisfaction. The CEO scorecard reflected the performance of the bank as a whole and this was shared in town halls to showcase the progress made by the bank towards the mission.

To drive the culture of data-based management and decision-making, one of the techniques used by DBS was that no business review would be carried out with presentations and reports put together by the teams. Instead, dashboards generated by their digital systems were seen as the source of truth. These dashboards were fed by the transactional systems, so the data was current, and it enabled analysis and visualization of the business progress, thus enabling quick and effective decision-making.

Most large transformations tend to take a measured approach. Piloting, measuring success and reviewing plans are the most preferred options. Several manufacturing organizations have been applying elements of Industry 4.0 to bring about improvement in efficiencies, quality and cost. Most of them use the concept of lighthouse facilities—one of the manufacturing sites, wherein they pilot a combination of these transformations, measures the outcome before rolling out. One of the challenges that have been observed is very long pilot durations, which leads to fatigue. It makes sense to have a tight, time-bound pilot followed by the roll-out, or else the full benefits of transformation may not be realized. A good strategy would be to 'crawl–walk–run'.

In summary, digital transformation is a very exciting and impactful journey which can provide significant benefits to an organization. It can make the organization much more competitive, agile and economically successful. However, it is also a journey that needs to be planned very meticulously and must be undertaken with a mission. It is not a short and quick exercise, but is likely to be a multi-year programme, needing support from various stakeholders.

Case Study on Digital Transformation: Axis Bank Digital Transformation

Axis Bank is India's third largest private sector bank. Founded in 1993, Axis is a universal bank with activities across retail, corporate, SME and government segments. In 2019, Axis Bank witnessed a senior management transition with a new CEO, Amitabh Chaudhry, taking charge at the helm. The bank unveiled its Growth Profitability Sustainability (GPS) strategy with an aspiration of delivering 18 per cent RoE sustainably, while delivering growth above industry rates. One of the key elements of the GPS strategy was to set up a digital bank within the bank and to leverage this to transform the core bank. With this aspiration in mind, the bank set up a new team—Digital Business and Transformation (DBAT). DBAT was set up with a couple of mandates in mind.

First, DBAT was to establish and deliver Open by Axis. Open by Axis would include all the business that is done completely end-to-end digitally without any human intervention. Every part of the life cycle would be delivered digitally starting from digital marketing, application, underwriting, operations and so on. This would require building new product journeys which could be done 100 per cent in do-it-yourself mode by customers.

Second, DBAT would extend journeys that they build for Open by Axis to the core franchise, enabling physical teams (e.g., branch, outbound call centres) to source business and service customers leveraging digital. This would enable teams to be more effective and productive thanks to simpler customer journeys, elimination of paper, significantly lower turnaround times, etc.

Delivering a digital proposition that could compete in the fast-evolving fintech space would require fundamental changes and would not be easy. To do this, the bank made a few strategic choices. First, the bank decided to set up DBAT as a business unit—with targets for business, costs, risks, etc. While the targets were shadowed with core businesses, this enabled the bank to take a business-led lens to digital transformation. Second, the bank decided to build in-house proprietary digital capabilities. In a world where the quality of digital journeys, design and engineering provide a distinctive competitive edge, it was evident that creating an in-house capability for all these functions was essential. Consequently, the digital team in the bank expanded from about sixty in 2019 to over 2500 by 2023. The DBAT team itself grew to ~750 and included a 350-member engineering team, a fifty-member design team, and 300 digital product managers and digital marketing experts.

With the team in place, the bank invested in setting up an advanced operating model. All digital journeys were delivered via Pods—a cross-functional team comprising individuals from the digital team, engineering and IT, core product team, risk, compliance, operations, etc. This team would be entrusted with the successful delivery of the product. This ensured that all views came on the table right upfront at design and also hastened the process of getting and incorporating feedback. Each journey started with a clear definition of end outcomes and the delivery of metrics was tracked rigorously to ensure that the Pods stayed true to business outcomes

No amount of front-end beautification would deliver true transformation unless the core tech delivered flexibility, stability and scale. To achieve this, the bank initiated major tech investments in parallel to the digital built. APIs were exposed from core systems via an Enterprise Service Bus to enable the decoupling of front-end systems from core systems and to speed up front-end delivery. Several core banking systems were upgraded. The resilience of tech systems became a major initiative, and several changes were made, including upgrading hardware, introducing monitoring systems, automating deployments, establishing processes for discovering issues and remediating them in case of downtimes, etc. The bank decided to adopt cloud and was the first mover in the country in this process. Between 2020 and 2023, 30 per cent of legacy applications were moved to the cloud; further, almost all new customer-facing applications, launched post-2020, were cloud native. Axis was considered a benchmark bank when it came to cloud adoption.

Building on top of the foundational tech and people capability, the bank built several proprietary capabilities and tools. As an example, the bank built its own design system called Subzero. This was an atomic design system with standardized design elements. Additionally, the code for these elements was available in a central system. Subzero helped reduce design time by 30 per cent and also enhanced engineering productivity. All new applications in the bank were built using Subzero— this enabled consistency of design across journeys. The bank also put in place a Continuous Integration and Continuous Deployment (CI/CD) and DevSecOps pipeline. This automated large parts of the software development and deployment life cycle, including security checks. With this, the bank moved to an agile development methodology with an integrated product and engineering team. Also, this significantly helped expand the deployment capacity of the bank, making it 24x7; at the same time, it reduced deployment errors dramatically. Finally, the bank built in several micro-services which followed the build-once-use-multiple-times philosophy. [3]

In addition to tech, the ability to leverage data would be critical to success in digital. Towards this, the bank took several steps to strengthen and create leadership in analytics. These included introducing and scaling tech systems such as a big data lake, personalization architecture, real-time analytics driven decision-making, e.g., for underwriting, marketing and personalization. Several new tools and technologies were introduced to enable real-time data ingestion (e.g., Kafka), data quality and discoverability (e.g., Informatica MDM), data engineering workloads (e.g., Cloudera), enabling data as a service (DynamoDB, Mongo DB) and real-time models and decisions (e.g., Blaze). The bank built a strong data science team which built models for various use cases, including underwriting, fraud identification, next product to buy, income estimation, etc.

With a significant capability built under its belt, the bank worked on delivering business outcomes. Over thirty

---

[3] DevSecOps is a modern software development practice that integrates security into every stage of the DevOps process, from initial design through to deployment. The goal is to automate and embed security testing and monitoring within the development pipeline, ensuring that software is both delivered quickly and safeguarded against vulnerabilities.

new customer journeys were launched across products and customer segments. By 2023, ~5 per cent of the bank's business came via Open by Axis. The impact of Open by Axis and core transformation was seen across the bank. Open by Axis contributed ~60 per cent to fixed deposits, ~50 per cent to new mutual fund sales, 23 per cent to personal loans, 24 per cent to credit cards and so on. Further, considering assisted business, these numbers were even higher—more than 50 per cent for all the products listed above. In terms of services, ~70 per cent of all service requests were now serviced via Open by Axis. Digital journeys delivered significantly better customer experiences— NPS for digital products were between 5 to 30 percentage points better, compared with their physical counterparts. Finally, Open by Axis also delivered better economic outcomes. Across most products, the cost of acquisition and the cost of processing were both better, compared with physical journeys.

Open by Axis also enabled the bank to deliver significant customer engagement benefits. Open by Axis, the bank's mobile app, was rated 4.8 on both the Google Play Store and the iOS App Store. With over 2.4 million reviews, it was the highest rated mobile banking app in the world on the Playstore.[4] Across metrics such as MAU, transactions, services delivered and products sold, Open by Axis witnessed strong growth of 2–8x, between 2019 and 2023.[5]

The bank also launched several initiatives to work with the broader ecosystem. Axis Bank is a leader in digital partnerships.

---

[4] Based on a comparison of app ratings of the top 500 banks by market capitalization, as on 30 Sep 2023.

[5] *Axis Bank*, November 13, 2024, www.axisbank.com

It has strong partnerships in the area of UPI (market share of 16 per cent), credit cards (over 3 million cards sourced via partners), loans, among others. The bank is a preferred partner for industry-leading ecosystem players such as Flipkart (e-commerce), Google Pay (payments), Samsung (devices), Amazon (e-commerce/payments), PhonePe (payments), among others. The bank was also a leader in leveraging ecosystem enablers. India now has an emerging Account Aggregator ecosystem, which enables customers, with their consent, to share their financial information, such as bank statements, digitally, with other institutions. Axis was the first bank to go live on the ecosystem. Today, the bank offers multiple types of loans and credit cards using Account Aggregator data. The bank also allows customers to create a one-view of their balances across banks. The RBI Innovation Hub, a central bank subsidiary, introduced a Tech Platform for Frictionless Credit with various information sources being offered such as land records. The bank was also among the first to work with the platform.

Finally, the bank built several tools to enable its physical teams. One Axis—an app to manage everyday work was rolled out to the entire employee base. Siddhi—a one-stop platform for all frontline teams, enabling them to service and sell new products, was launched. In addition to product and service journeys, Siddhi provided a number of productivity enhancing capabilities to the staff. These included personalized nudges, the ability to manage and view the team's performance on input and output metrics, the view of performance across products, calendars for customer meets, etc.

Key Takeaways

1. Understanding Digital Transformation:
   - Digitization: The initial step of converting data into digital form to improve storage, retrieval and localized process efficiency.
   - Digitalization: Using digital technology to change processes, making them more agile, better quality and lower cost, but not necessarily transforming the business.
   - Digital Transformation: Utilizing digital technology across various aspects of a business to fundamentally change operations and value delivery, aiming to enhance competitiveness, customer experience and agility.

2. Timing for Transformation:
   - The last decade's technological advancements (cloud computing, data analytics, IoT, AI) have provided businesses with opportunities to reimagine their offerings.
   - Customer expectations have dramatically increased, driven by widespread smartphone adoption and experiences in gaming, shopping, healthcare and education.
   - A new competitive landscape with digital-first or digital-only players, offering frictionless solutions at lower operational costs, has emerged.

3. Key Dimensions of Digital Transformation:
   - New Product Offerings: Digital technologies enable new product offerings, such as end-to-end digital banking services and online payment systems like UPI.
   - Process Reimagination: Technologies can improve or entirely reimagine processes, such as using IoT for supply chain management to optimize inventory and reduce stock-outs.

- Customer Experience: Digital journeys capture valuable data to customize and enhance customer experience, reducing friction and increasing revenue.

4. Framework for Transformation:
   - Understanding the Current Business Model: Use tools like the Business Model Canvas, SWOT analysis and feedback from customers and employees to assess the current state and identify opportunities.
   - Identifying Transformation Opportunities: Focus on customer-centric opportunities, operational efficiencies, product and service innovation, and market expansion.
   - Leveraging Technology: Stay updated with new technologies to drive transformation, such as generative AI for customer contact centres and big data analytics for personalization and real-time decision-making.

5. Implementing the Transformation:
   - Starting with Appropriate Opportunities: Assess the current technological landscape and identify feasible opportunities for transformation.
   - Creating an Enabling Environment: Align the organization with the transformation vision through strong leadership, continuous communication and change management initiatives.
   - Driving Change: Measure and share progress continuously, using data-driven decision-making and piloting initiatives to ensure successful implementation.

6. Case Studies:
   - Axis Bank: A comprehensive example of digital transformation involving the setting up of a digital business unit, building proprietary digital capabilities,

adopting cloud technologies and leveraging data analytics to deliver superior customer experiences and operational efficiencies.

Digital transformation is a strategic, multi-year journey that requires meticulous planning, robust leadership and a strong alignment across the organization. By embracing digital technologies, businesses can achieve significant improvements in competitiveness, agility and economic success. However, this transformation must be approached with a clear vision, continuous measurement and a commitment to data-driven decision-making to ensure sustainable growth and adaptation in a rapidly evolving digital landscape.

Acknowledgements

They say it takes a village to raise a child, and after spending the last year working on this book, I realize the same is true for writing one. I am deeply grateful to everyone who has shaped my journey in entrepreneurship, management and this writing endeavour.

First and foremost, I would like to express my heartfelt gratitude to my wife, Meena Ganesh—a serial entrepreneur and inspiring leader. Her deep understanding of business models and her contributions to sections of this book have been invaluable. To my daughter, Akshita Ganesh, for enriching the chapters on platforms and marketplaces, and my son, Atishay Ganesh, for his guidance on technology and digital innovations.

I extend special gratitude to my co-founders across four ventures including Karan Puri, Hemant Kohli, Ajay Row, Sanjiv Dalal, Ramki, Vinay Misra, Shankar Maruwada and Srini Rai, who have been invaluable partners in my entrepreneurial journey.

To the founders of GrowthStory companies—your dedication and hard work have been instrumental in shaping my thinking. Special mention to Sudhakar, Hari Menon and Vipul Parekh from BigBasket, Vaibhav Tiwari from Portea Medical, Gaurav Singh Kushwaha from BlueStone and Srikanth Iyer from HomeLane.

I am grateful to IIM Bangalore and the Indian School of Business for the opportunity to teach business model innovation and entrepreneurship, a truly rewarding experience. Many chapters in this book have evolved from my discussions with students and faculty.

A special note of gratitude goes to Manish Kumar, senior commissioning editor at Penguin Random House India, for his patience and guidance in teaching a novice like me the fundamentals of writing a book.

Thanks to Nandan Nilekani, an inspiring role model, for graciously agreeing to review and comment on this book. I also extend my thanks to Sriharsha Majety (Swiggy), Vijay Shekhar Sharma (Paytm) and Professor Rishikesha Krishnan (director, IIM Bangalore) for providing their invaluable feedback and comments. A special thanks to Shiv Shivakumar (ex-chairman Pepsico and ex-CEO, emerging markets, Nokia) for reviewing the manuscript and writing the foreword.

To everyone who has supported, inspired and guided me along the way—thank you.

Scan QR code to access the
Penguin Random House India website